FOR THE
FIRST TIME ON
TELEVISION

TO LINDA –
NICE MEETING You!

–Gary Berman

FOR THE
FIRST TIME ON
TELEVISION

by Garry Berman

Published in the USA by:
BearManor Media
P O Box 71426
Albany, Georgia 31708
www.bearmanormedia.com

Printed in the United States of America
ISBN   978-1-59393-929-8 (paperback)
         978-1-59393-930-4 (hardcover)

Book & cover design and layout by Darlene Swanson • www.van-garde.com

CONTENTS

Chapter 3: The Technological Firsts

Chapter 4: Firsts in Television News Coverage

Chapter 5: Firsts in Coverage of Political Events

Chapter 6: Firsts in Sports Coverage

Chapter 7: Miscellaneous Firsts

ACKNOWLEDGMENTS

All photos are taken from the author's personal collection.

Many thanks to the following individuals for their assistance in preparing this book: David C. Tucker, Billy Ingram, Ben Ohmart, and Darlene Swanson.

Thanks also to the good people at Panera Bread in Moorestown, and Mt. Laurel, New Jersey--including Lexie, Jonathan, Maria, Steve, Tish, Ree, Jayla, and everyone else--who have made me feel so welcome, as I've sat with my frozen mocha drinks and sandwiches several times a week, while working on this book.

Finally, my deepest thanks to my wife Karen, who is hoping she can retire when this book makes me rich and famous.

This book is dedicated to my fellow TV addicts everywhere.

INTRODUCTION:
FIRST THINGS FIRST

Regardless of who you are, where you live, or what you do, chances are pretty good that you watch television, at least part of each day and/or evening. Maybe it's a few minutes of early-morning news on the way out the door, and a few sitcoms, police procedurals, or a reality competition show in the evening. Even in this computer/digital/virtual age, television is still the medium to which we turn when we're at home and want instant entertainment or information.

Americans simply like television, even those who may not readily admit it or claim that it's all "junk." But, of course, it's never been all junk. Much of it is really quite good. Some of it is brilliant. There's been good and bad television ever since Day One.

And speaking of Day One...

While most of us can claim a fairly extensive familiarity with a good deal of television, very few of us are aware of *when*, what, and under what circumstances, each onscreen television milestone first took place.

For a culture that has embraced television as we have for the past six decades, how many of us really know anything about the very first American sitcom—or the first reality show, science fiction series, or made-for-TV movie? We watch live news reports and sporting events as they happen around the world, but do we know the story of the very first news bulletin ever on television? Or the first time Instant Replay was used? Most of us have no idea. But the answers—as addictive as they are fascinating—can be found on the pages of this book.

It takes only a moment of pondering such questions as, say, when the first TV program was broadcast in color, or what the first-ever medical drama was, to realize how little we really know about the history of the medium that entertains us, informs us, and keeps us company at some point during each day and night. For everyone who has grown up since the end of World War II, television has become a constant, even integral part of our lives. And, of course, those of a certain age often watch today's television to recapture the enjoyment and memories provided by *yesterday's* television. Nostalgia television networks, such as MeTV, Antenna TV, Cozi, Decades, and others, have been giving baby-boomers what they want: extended trips down memory lane, encompassing about sixty-five years (give or take a few) of sitcoms, dramas, game shows, you name it. Viewers see many TV "firsts" on those channels, but often without even realizing it.

For the sake of historical accuracy and fairness, you will notice on these pages that many TV topics regarding who or what was the "first" tend to have more than one clear-cut answer. In addition, the line between early experimental TV transmissions—aired primarily for the benefit of lab technicians attempting to refine the technology—and proper broadcasts for public consumption (which consisted of little more than a handful of private citizens in the earliest days) can be a very, well, blurry one. But the distinction will be noted in each instance. It could be argued, then, that some examples of TV firsts "don't count" because they did not occur on broadcasts that would have any real viewing audience. However, the examples cited in the text have been deemed significant enough milestones in television's overall timeline to warrant their inclusion.

For instance, it's fair to ask if a brief dramatic scene, transmitted from a crude TV studio in Rockefeller Center in New York to an equally crude receiver just a few floors below in the same building, and seen only by technicians, would count as a "broadcast," and worthy of being considered the "first" of anything. To paraphrase the cliché, if a televised tree falls in a televised forest in 1936, but there's no one sitting in a private home with their own TV set to see or hear it, has it really fallen?

In compiling the firsts listed in this book, I've chosen those that are the most commonly accepted by television and pop culture historians. But there is often room for argument, and the inevitable "Ah, ha! You didn't mention the 'Uncle Ollie' kiddie program broadcast from the studio in Podunk, Name-A-State in 1945!" or some such admonishment. Well, that could be true. But if there isn't substantial enough reason to consider it a truly significant television first, then it won't be found on these pages.

CHAPTER 1
IN THE BEGINNING...

The story of how television was invented, where it was invented, and by whom, is a long one, with a populous cast. Television is commonly thought of as a post-World War II creation that began to hit its stride—in technology, content, and popularity—in the early 1950s. So, it may come as a surprise that television's practical development, or pre-history, dates back to the mid-1920s, when its older sibling, radio, was itself still a young medium.

In 1880, German inventor Paul Nipkow devised the apparatus on which the first successful early television experiments were based. The "Nipkow disk" was a metallic scanning disk with a spiral pattern of holes punched in it which was set before a brightly lighted subject or picture. As the disk spun at a high speed, the first hole would cross the picture at the top. The second hole passed across the picture a little lower down, the third hole lower than that. Upon completing a single revolution, the entire picture would be briefly exposed. The disk revolved fast enough to accomplish the scanning within one-fifteenth of a second.

Nipkow's device used lenses and mirrors to guide the light passing through the holes in the disk to a light-sensitive selenium cell. A dark area of the picture would cause a weak current to flow from the cell, a bright area caused a strong current, and the gray areas would trigger an intermediate current flow. These variations in the current were carried by a wire to a lamp, which changed its brightness according to the current. A second scanning disk in front of the lamp, and revolving at the same speed as the first one, allowed an observer looking at the flickering lamp through the disk to see a reproduction of the original picture.

To illustrate how experimental—but working—television dates back to the early days of radio, consider that the same year NBC created the first national radio network in 1926, the first true experiments to transmit moving images through the air, sometimes with sound, were taking place in Britain, America, and Germany. As many as a half-dozen individuals can be credited with playing a major part in inventing television, and the argument concerning who should receive top credit will probably continue in perpetuity. However, as is the case with most successful inventions, television is the product of their cumulative efforts.

Several inventors, working independently of each other with their own modified and improved versions of the Nipkow disk, made considerable progress in the early 1920s. The most prominent of these was young Scotsman John Logie Baird, who first demonstrated the transmission of live, moving images from a transmitter to a receiver. Baird gave the first of his demonstrations in March and April of 1925 in London's Selfridges department store. However, the images were merely moving silhouettes, without detail, significant contrast, or gray scale. Just a few months later, on June 13, Charles Francis Jenkins transmitted moving images through the air as well—including a silhouette of a small windmill—across Washington, D.C. over a distance of about five miles. His demonstration made the front page of *The New York Times* the following day.

The first person ever to appear on a TV screen

Early television transmissions of handmade signs and inanimate objects were all well and good at first, but television's real potential couldn't be truly demonstrated unless viewers could see the image of a real, live person sent from point A to point B.

You would think the first person ever to appear on television would have become a household name around the world, like others who have achieved famous firsts, such as Alexander Graham Bell, the Wright Brothers, or Neil Armstrong. And yet history has somehow allowed William Edward Taynton to fall through the cracks.

John Logie Baird

On October 2, 1925, John Logie Baird, working feverishly in his attic lab on Frith Street in the Soho section of London, used a popular ventriloquist dummy named "Stooky Bill" as his experimental television subject. He succeeded in transmitting an image of the dummy's head as a 30-line, vertically scanned picture, at five pictures per second, to his receiver, just a few feet across the room. Under an array of intense lighting, it was the first picture transmitted with a grayscale, allowing for variations of black-and-white image intensity, rather than appearing as a simple silhouette devoid of any detail.

Baird quickly decided that he wanted to see a live person's image transmitted, so he hurried downstairs to the office below in which twenty-year-old clerk William Taynton was working. Taynton had expressed an interest in Baird's experiments, so the inventor invited the lad to pose as the next televised subject, replacing Stooky Bill. After Taynton's face appeared on the receiver screen, Baird then took his own turn at the seat directly in front of his transmitting mechanism.

Word of Baird's series of successful attempts to transmit discernable, live images reached the U.S. in January of 1926. On January 23, *The New York Times* reported from London, "John L. Baird, who has perfected television after years of research, has been giving practical demonstrations here . . . " Just days later, on January 26, Baird demonstrated his apparatus for members of the Royal Institution and the press.

The first known modern-day use of the word "television"

It's plain to see, when dividing the word "television" in half, that its basic meaning is "to see at a distance ("tele" derived from Greek, and "vision" from Latin). Of course, there are plenty of words in English conveying similar meanings and concepts: telescope, telegraph, telephone, etc.

But when did the term "television," as we know it today, first begin making the rounds?

The idea of seeing distant images illuminated on a screen or other device had been the fancy of scientists and science fiction writers for a number of years by the turn of the twentieth century. But Russian scientist Constantin Perskyi is credited with coining the term "television" during his presentation at the 1900 Paris World's Fair, where he described, before the International Congress of Electricity, the efforts of Nipkow and others experimenting with photo-electric cells. Perskyi's use of the word "television," however, emerged as the result of a string of translations from German to Russian to French, and finally reported in English in *The Electrician* magazine.

When John Logie Baird made his first breakthroughs in 1925 and 1926, he referred to his device as a "televisor." However, Alfred Dinsdale, British journalist and member of the Radio Society of Great Britain, wrote in his 1926 book *Television: Seeing by Wireless* that several letters had been appearing in the press objecting to the mix of Greek and Latin to create the word. "These objections, however, come too late," he wrote, "the word 'television' is already part of the English language, and may be briefly defined as 'vision by telegraphy.'"

Two years later, Dinsdale became the founding editor of *Television* magazine, in which he explained:

Television is usually rather loosely defined as "seeing by wireless," for that is the popular term under which it so frequently masquerades. This is, however, hardly correct, for the television is seeing by *telegraphy*, either with or without wires. The Patent Office, which defines such terms, makes this quite clear by correctly laying down that television apparatus is that used for "transmitting instantaneously to a distance images of views, scenes, or objects by telegraphy, either wire or wireless."... Even Webster's Dictionary confuses television and photo-telegraphy, but it should be clearly understood that the one refers to vision of living scenes at the moment of them taking place and the other to the mere sending of a "still" picture.

Another early television pioneer, Charles Francis Jenkins, used the term "radio vision."

And the word "radioscope," (sometimes one word, sometimes two) was also used to describe the invention. The terms "motion picture broadcasting" and "radio-television" were common as well, into the early 1930s, when both laymen as well as seasoned journalists were still finding themselves grappling for the best descriptive term. But by 1930, "television" had pretty much gained the greatest acceptance among those who were still developing the technology and steering its future. Just as importantly, it became the standard noun used in magazines and newspapers, where the masses turned to follow its evolution from a simple experiment to a promising new medium.

But even as that particular issue appeared to be settled, another question arose as to what the proper word should be to ascribe to the person who *watches* television. The word "viewer" seems obvious to us today, but in April of 1931, there were a good number of interesting suggestions submitted by request to the *New York Times* from all over the country. Among those were: "visual listener," "sightener," "televiewer," and "scanner." J.W.Horton of the General Radio Company did indeed suggest "viewer," and radio pioneer Dr. Lee DeForest offered "televiewer" and "teleseer." But we can be grateful that D.E. Repogle, of the Jenkins Television Corporation, did not find acceptance for his suggestion, "looker-in."

In fact, *Television News* magazine held a contest of its own in 1931, inviting readers to submit a replacement for "looker-in." The publication offered a $50.00 prize for the winner, and later claimed to have received several thousand entries. "So many people participated in the contest, it would seem more or less necessary that a really adequate word should be found to replace the cumbersome one 'lookers-in.'" Some of the more eye-catching, even poetic, suggestions included "teleseer," "visagers," and "scan-fans". The winning entry came from Sidney Karl Steinfeld of New Orleans, for the world "visualist." It was explained that "the word was selected because it was euphonious and expressed exactly what it is supposed to. Sitting in front of a television receiver you visualize the image before you; this, consequently, makes you a visualist. But, as we have said at the beginning, it may be doubtful that the word finds its way into the common language. Only time can tell."

And time did indeed determine that "visualist" was not a keeper.

The first long-distance television transmission

The first major television breakthrough in America came on April 27, 1927, when engineers at AT&T Labs achieved the first live inter-city television transmission by wire. The experiment linked Commerce Secretary (and future president) Herbert Hoover in Washington, D.C., and AT&T president Walter Gifford in New York, about 230 miles away.

The experiment took place in two stages—first with a transmission by wire, using telephone lines from Washington, D.C. to New York City, and then an over-the-air broadcast from the Whippany, New Jersey, transmitter and studio to New York.

The first person to appear to those watching was a young female telephone operator, since the audio was supplied by phone. Even though the group in New York could see and hear those on the Washington end, the visuals were sent only one way. The girl in Washington appeared on the screen and, as if placing a normal phone call, asked to whom Gifford wished to speak. Gifford then launched into this speech:

Today we are to witness another milestone in the conquest of nature by science. We shall see the fruition of years of study on the problem of seeing at a distance as though face to face. The principles underlying television, which are related to the principles involved in electrical transmission of speech, have been known for a long time, but today we shall demonstrate its successful achievement. The elaborateness of the equipment required by the very nature of the undertaking precludes any present possibility of television being available in homes and offices generally. What its practical use may be I shall leave to your imagination. I am confident, however, that in many ways, and in due time, it will be found to add substantially to human comfort and happiness.

General J.J. Carty, in Washington, then took a seat before the televisor, and indicated for the demonstration to begin. He held a telephone speaking end in his hand while the light of an arc lamp flickered on his face. As described

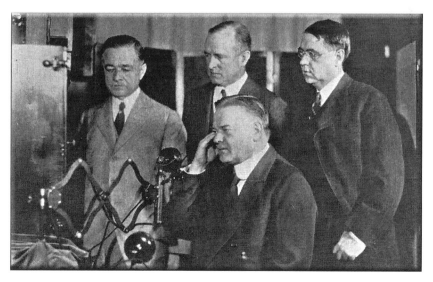

Herbert Hoover participates in America's first long-distance television transmission.

at the time, "Small dots of light are moving across his face, one after another, but at such high speed that they bathe his countenance in uniform illumination that has a bluish tinge. These lights are dissecting his face into small squares. And each tiny part travels over the wire to New York with inconceivable rapidity; in fact, at the rate of 45,000 a second. The receiver reassembles the squares as a mosaic. It takes about 2,500 of the tiny squares or 'units,' as they are called to build up each complete pictures."

The two men exchanged greetings before Carty relinquished his seat to Hoover, who, at first, leaned too far forward, in such a way that his forehead took up too much of the picture. He also held his telephone too close to his mouth and chin, but then adjusted his position, allowing his image to be more easily recognized. He then offered his first words regarding the occasion:

"It is a matter of just pride to have a part in this historic occasion. We have long been familiar with the electrical transmission of sound. Today we have, in a sense, the transmission of sight, for the first time in the world's history . . . "

His image was satisfactory on the small screen, but when enlarged to a 2 x 3 foot projection, much of the clarity was lost. However, journalist Orrin Dunlop couldn't contain his excitement. "This is a triumph for television," he wrote. "The New Yorkers are thrilled to see the image come to life, as it begins to talk, smile, nod its head and look this way and that."

Once this exchange between Washington and New York was accomplished via telephone wire, the next portion of the demonstration involved an over-the-air transmission, originating from the AT&T transmitter in Whippany, New Jersey. From there, the first face to appear on the screen was that of E.L. Nelson, an engineer who provided his viewers with a technical explanation of what was taking place.

Nelson was followed by a vaudeville comedian identified as A. Dolan, who performed a monologue in a brogue, sporting side whiskers and a broken pipe. He then left his place in front of the transmitter, but appeared a few minutes later in black face, telling jokes in a "negro" dialect. By doing so, he became the first comedian ever to appear on a television transmission, "And in its possibilities," wrote Dunlop, "an observer compares it with the Fred Ott sneeze of more than thirty years ago, the first piece of comedy recorded in the movies."

After Dolan, Mrs. H.A. Frederick of Mountain Lakes, New Jersey, offered a short humorous dialect talk of her own. Before and between the acts an announcer also made an appearance to speak a few words.

The experiment was indeed an early triumph of television, the first of its kind in America. But only a month later, back in the U.K., Baird exceeded the 230-mile distance by sending a television signal via a telephone line, over 438 miles, from London to Glasgow.

The first television station in the U.S.

Advances in television development occurred at a quickening pace in the mid to late 1920s, with several major milestones taking place in 1928 alone. Bear in mind that these advances were happening even as motion pictures were still making their own first steps into the sound era (with *The Jazz Singer* released in 1927 and *The Lights of New York* in 1928).

The first television station in America was born in the somewhat unlikely locale of Schenectady, New York. Why Schenectady? In the 1920s, it was the home of General Electric's labs, from which television pioneer E. F. W. Alexanderson initiated the country's first over-the-air transmission for the public on January 13, 1928.

On that day, David Sarnoff, general manager of RCA, told a handful of his invited guests that they were about to witness the demonstration of "an epoch-making development." It was an event, he suggested, like the demonstration of wireless telegraphy by Marconi.

G.E. company officials, engineers, and newspapermen were then ushered into a darkened room and crowded around two wooden receiving cabinets, each a little more than four feet high and much resembling phonograph cabinets. Each cabinet housed a 3" x 3" screen. As the experiment began, the voice of Leslie Wilkins, of the General Electric testing department, came from the loud-speaker next to one of the cabinets. "I understand there is an audience in the receiving room now," he said from the alcove where he was broadcasting, "so now we will start."

The image of his face then appeared, often floating back and forth slowly across the field of view, but it did come in clearly enough for details to be visible, including small gestures. He took off his glasses, put them back on again, and blew a smoke ring.

The group then heard and saw on the screen a succession of individuals addressing the transmitter from that section of the laboratory. In addition, and even more importantly, other groups gathered around receiving sets in the private homes of E.W. Allen, Vice President of the General Electric Company in charge of engineering; Edwin W. Rice, Jr., Honorary President of the board of the company; and Dr. Alexanderson.

The next person to appear on the screen was Louis Dean, the regular announcer of WGY, who offered his rendition of "Ain't She Sweet?" accompanying himself on his ukulele.

Witnesses reported that the picture of each performer was not steadily maintained, and continued to shift left and right. If the image went too far to one side, another, identical image appeared alongside the first.

The program continued for over two hours, as the signal covered roughly a twenty-mile radius, and was received on all of four home TV sets, each with a screen only half the size of the receiver monitor in the lab.

The following day, *The New York Times* declared in its front-page story that the successful broadcast "heralded another human conquest of space. Sent through the air like the voice which accompanied the picture, it marked, the demonstrators declared, the first demonstration of television broadcasting and gave the first absolute proof of the possibility of connecting homes throughout the world by sight as they have already been connected by voice."

Sarnoff boldly predicted, even at that early stage, that television would eventually become a common fixture in the American household. Even with his P.T. Barnum-like penchant for hyperbole, he was quite on point when he promised, "The television receiver, as at present developed, will supplement and replace the modern radio receiving set in the home. Broadcasting of television, it seems clear, will develop along parallel lines with broadcasting of sound, so that eventually not only sound but also sight through radio broadcasting will be available to every home."

Word of the success even spread quickly across the ocean. In the first issue of Britain's *Television* magazine, editor Alfred Dinsdale broke the news to his readers:

"It is part of our policy to give our readers detailed technical descriptions of the apparatus and methods used by experimenters the whole world over. For example, as we write these lines a newspaper dispatch informs us that the General Electric Company, of Schenectady, N.Y., has just succeeded in broadcasting television, through the world-famous broadcasting station, WGY, to four private homes. This means that the home television set is already in sight."

The Schenectady station's original call letters at the time were W2XB, but was often referred to as WGY, the call letters of the GE-owned sister radio station there. Many in the area referred to the fledgling TV station as "WGY television." The station went through a few other temporary sets of call letters before the year was over. In 1939, as W2XB once again, it began its affiliation with W2XBS (NBC-owned) in New York, becoming the first affiliate of the NBC television network. (Side note: In 1941, the first year of commercial TV broadcasting in the U.S., the station moved into the first TV studio in the country to be specifically designed as a TV studio. The following year the call letters became WRGB. In 1981, WRGB became a CBS affiliate, and today continues to be the oldest continually operating TV station in the world.)

On July 2, 1928, about six months after the landmark experiment in Schenectady, station W3XK began broadcasting from suburban Washington, D.C. The station was an outgrowth of the experimental lab work done by inventor Charles Francis Jenkins. He sold several thousand receiving sets, mostly to hobbyists, and, after receiving permission to start an experimental TV transmitting station, began to air programming five nights a week, making W3XK the first station in the country to do so. The station ceased operations in 1932, but by then Jenkins had opened a new experimental studio in New York.

Back in the U.K., on July 22, 1928, Baird demonstrated perhaps the most astounding of his many inventions of the time. It would not become a consumer item available to the public for another fifty years (in a much more refined form, of course), but he did indeed invent and successfully demonstrate what we would know today as a video disk. He accomplished this by taking a phonograph record and creating a double groove—one to reproduce sound and another to carry moving images in synchronization with that sound—to be seen on his receiving screen. While he did succeed in creating the working system, which he dubbed "phonovision," it clearly needed more work than he was prepared to devote at the time. But, as we know, video disks first hit the market in the late 1970s, and played in a manner similar to that of phonograph records, à la Baird's breakthrough—before laser technology brought us the CD and DVD.

By the early 1930s, it was clear that the Nipkow disk's early successes had succumbed to mechanical limitations that simply couldn't be overcome, despite the considerable efforts by technicians and engineers determined to improve the system. A young American inventor, Philo Farnsworth, recognized the inherent limitations of the disk and its mechanical means to transmit images, and sought to devise a superior, electronic process.

On September 7, 1927, Farnsworth, working at his lab on Green Street in San Francisco, used his image dissenter camera to transmit its first image, a straight line. The first public demonstration took place on September 3, 1928, during which Farnsworth's camera transmitted a dollar sign. The following year, he refined the equipment still more, eliminating the motor generator, thereby creating an *all-electronic* TV camera, with no mechanical parts. This effectively rendered the Nipkow disk—even its updated versions—obsolete.

Moving along the timeline, NBC opened an experimental TV transmitter in New York in 1930, and by the following year, in Chicago, about a thousand sets were reported to be in use. The Western Television Corporation there offered two to three hours entertainment each day, over local W9XAO. Visual acts were the most popular, such as fire-eaters, acrobats, circus clowns and jugglers. The Chicago *Daily News* also operated an experimental station, W9XAP, which cost about $4,000 a year to run. The overseeing regulatory body at the time, the Federal Radio Commission, had banned television advertising, so early station owners needed to have fairly deep pockets to stay on the air.

In 1931, what could be described as the first two-way video chat ever took place in New York City between novelist Fannie Hurst and her husband. While she sat in a small booth directly facing the TV camera at the AT&T building, he sat in an identical booth at the Bell laboratories five miles away. Whether or not there was an audio component to the connection is unclear (if so, it would have been via telephone line), but the spouses, at the very least, smiled and waved to each other for the transmission. Hurst described it as "the greatest thrill of an eventful life."

Meanwhile, as far as TV for the general public was concerned, the television audience of 1932 was estimated by *Variety* magazine to be about 30,000 nationwide, with twelve 50-kilowatt television transmitting stations dotted across the country.

Overseas, engineers in both Germany and Great Britain kept vigilant of each other's progress. In Germany, with the Nazi party's power already omnipotent, all early television experiments were conducted under the party's auspices. Electronic cameras there had been in use since March 22, 1935, the birth date of German TV. Even so, the picture quality was poor, due mostly to the rush to beat the U.K. and U.S. The first regular TV broadcasts consisted largely of Nazi propaganda programs, and, while they were on the air three times a week, the equipment permitted only head and shoulder shots of those seated in a closet-like scanning cell. These shows were all televised live, broadcast from the Paul Nipkow Television Station, a small studio in Berlin.

The disappointing picture quality prompted the Nazis to assign a television troupe to produce television content shot on 35mm film. The prominent program at this early stage was a propaganda series called *Strength Through Joy*. Another program, *Roof Garden*, was the first German entertainment show, consisting of musical acts and, of course, more Nazi propaganda. It had its broadcast premiere on June 19, 1935.

Since only party big shots, post office technicians, and some journalists owned televisions, viewing parlors were set up in Berlin, where about twenty people at a time could sit in a darkened room and watch one or two small-screened monitors in the front.

In Britain, 1936 was also a landmark year, during which the BBC agreed to experiment with both the mechanical Baird system and the Marconi-EMI electronic system, giving each equal consideration before choosing a standard for broadcasting. Part of Alexandra Palace in London was reconstructed to accommodate both production facilities and transmission equipment.

On August 26, television made its big splash at the Radiolympia Exhibition, where the public could see the first demonstrations. There were two one-hour transmissions each day for a ten-day period. The two systems were used alternately, and the program content included vaudeville acts, newsreels and documentary films from both Britain and America. The BBC estimated that more than 100,000 people visited the television booths. It officially inaugurated its television service on November 2, airing two hours a day, six days a week, for the next few months. By February of 1937, the Marconi-EMI system had been chosen over Baird's.

American progress at the time came about more slowly than that in Britain and Germany, but crude studios and control rooms, transmitting what amounted to "practice" productions—most notably by RCA in New York—did create the first broadcasts that a precious few receivers could pick up.

On July 7, 1936, RCA conducted an experimental broadcast, described as television's "first planned show," for invited guests and RCA licensees, who viewed the performance on specially-prepared receivers at Radio City. The ten-kilowatt transmitter atop the Empire State Building had opened a week before, prompting the RCA engineers to work overtime throughout the week to iron out the technical kinks and get an acceptable picture. Their work took them right up until 1:35 a.m. of the big day.

The event was filmed by Pathe News Inc., which set up a film camera about ten feet behind the studio TV camera (consequently, several of the acts were almost totally blocked from view of the film camera by the television equipment).

The first segment of the broadcast presented RCA president David Sarnoff and board chairman Major General J.G. Harbord, sitting at a desk on a simple studio set resembling an office. After some stilted dialogue between the two men, extolling the significance of the transmission, Sarnoff got up to leave the studio and join the invited viewers on the 62nd floor to watch the rest of the show.

The next hour consisted of a mix of short newsreel films, an outdoor ballet performance by the Radio City Music Hall Ballet, a fashion show, a comedy team performing in blackface, the Pickens Sisters singing and performing a comedic opera routine, and finally comedian Ed Wynn, who had been speaking frequently in interviews about his desire to appear on television. Just a few years before, he had been turning down numerous offers to star in his own radio show, mostly because he was more interested in performing on television, where both his verbal and visual comedy could be performed and appreciated as they had been for nearly thirty years.

Even after grudgingly accepting Texaco's astonishing offer of $5,000 a week to star as the "Fire Chief" on radio, Wynn continued to wait impatiently for television, hoping to "try to prove to the radio audience that if they think I am funny now, they will like me twice as well in television. I'm not saying this to be vain; I'm speaking purely from a professional viewpoint."

For his first opportunity to appear before a TV camera, however, Wynn awkwardly stepped in front of the camera, claiming that he had just been asked to participate in the production a half hour earlier, and thus had no prepared material. "I don't know what to say," he shrugged (whether or not this was merely an act is difficult to determine). Finally, his longtime announcer, Graham McNamee, appeared, seemingly to Wynn's relief, and the two got into some silly banter and visual riddles before the RCA broadcast was brought to a close.

In 1937, there were fewer than twenty experimental TV stations operating across the country, but the possibilities for TV broadcasting looked promising. Another celebrated experiment took place on June 7, 1938. Excerpts of the Broadway play *Susan and God,* starring Gertrude Lawrence, were performed and telecast from RCA studio 3H. Just over forty people watched on receiver elsewhere in Radio City, with perhaps another dozen watching at home in the New York City area. Producer John Golden introduced the 22-minute show. Positive reactions from both the audience and the press provided a big boost for TV's potential.

Show business reacts to television

Almost as soon as descriptions of the first public demonstrations of TV in England and America spread in the press throughout the late 1920s and early 1930s, the concept of radio-with-pictures grabbed the collective imagination of the public, and those in show business were not immune to the curiosity and growing excitement at television's potential. While scientists continued refining the technology behind television, those in the entertainment industry, who would ostensibly end up in front of the television camera at some undetermined point, couldn't help but ponder how the fledging medium might affect their careers, for better or worse.

Some stage actors, even one as well-respected as Lionel Barrymore, saw the coming of TV as yet another threat to the theater, close on the heels of sound motion pictures. In a 1928 interview, Barrymore said of films, "Pretty soon they will have color, talking, and the whole works in the movies. They are going to work it up until they have the whole business... It won't be long until movie actors will have to speak lines just as they do on the stage now. Then television will be the next thing, and we won't have to have any theatres at all."

By the following year, some current and future stars, such as Claudette Colbert, Jimmy Durante, Al Jolson, and Milton Berle, found themselves, at various times, in front of crude television equipment, and under intensely hot lights, as part of experimental tests. The likes of George Jessel, Sophie Tucker, and Ted Healy did likewise.

In his autobiography, Berle recalled his brief first time in front of a television camera, in 1929. F.A. Sanabria, owner of the United States Television Corporation in Chicago, asked Berle and Trixie Friganza to perform a portion of his stand-up routine as part of an experimental transmission. "My instructions were to do eight minutes and keep it clean, and don't move around too much. Of the actual broadcast, all I can remember is a small room and fierce heat from the lights and the heavy make-up we had to wear. We were part of history, but I don't think either of us made history. The broadcast was sent out to maybe twelve people in Sanabria's company who had sets."

Even at this early stage in television's development, a plethora of predictions and proposed uses for the medium began to appear with increasing frequency. Hugo Gernsback, editor of *Television News*, had his own interesting point of view, claiming that the "legitimate" theater was doomed, due to the popularity of movies and their comparatively inexpensive ticket prices. He proposed that television could be the solution, and put forth the concept of a specially-designed theater, with multiple sets in a circular layout, and the TV camera in the center. The plan would have a play's actors move from set to set, rather than taking breaks in between scenes to change the backgrounds. The televised plays from New York would be transmitted to projection screens in theaters across the country—thereby enabling theater audiences anywhere to see a Broadway production.

Another major star whose enthusiasm for television, like that of Ed Wynn's, far exceeded its technological progress in the early 1930s was none other than "America's Sweetheart," silent screen legend Mary Pickford, whose legendary silent screen career had made her arguably the most famous woman in the world. With the development of sound films, she dismissed talkies, and was quoted as saying, "putting sound on film would be like putting lipstick on the Venus de Milo." (Ironically, she won an Academy Award for her starring role in her first sound film, *Coquette*.)

Pickford retired from screen acting in 1933, but in contrast to her ambivalence about sound films, she could barely contain her enthusiasm for the promise of television. In 1934, she told the *Radio Mirror*, "Television is *not* a thing of the future. Another year will see it alongside radio in the home. It is no longer a matter of guess work. The inventors are certain it will go on the market as a popular instrument for entertainment before another twelve months go by."

So fervent was her excitement to get in on the ground floor of television that she signed to star in a series of radio broadcasts as a preparation for television, where she knew she would have to speak as part of her acting on a regular basis. To her, radio was to be her training ground for what she hoped to be a new career on the small screen.

"I guess I must be a pioneer," she mused. "Here is the whole new field of television and I want to see be the first to enter it. I'm terribly ambitious, you know." But despite her gushing words for the new medium throughout the 1930s, Pickford didn't step before a television camera until the 1953 Academy Awards broadcast.

Comedian and top radio star Eddie Cantor shared Mary Pickford's notion that radio could be used as a means to help performers adapt to television's anticipated demands. In November of 1936, he announced his intentions to begin the practice of memorizing his lines for radio, rather than relying on reading his scripts in front of the microphone each week. "Television will not be such a revolutionary change for the actor with stage and screen experience," he said, "but it will be a hard task-master for those radio artists whose personalities have remained hidden behind the unseeing 'mike.'"

In the months leading to television's official coming-out party at the 1939 World's Fair approached, Cantor was already among the ranks of stars eagerly awaiting its arrival: "Right now television is a reality in England. A wonderful reality. I know, I've seen it. I watched a golf match on a television screen, and saw a fellow miss an eight-foot putt. That's real enough for me."

Television's first "official" introduction to the American public

The April 30, 1939, opening of the World's Fair in New York served as the platform for David Sarnoff's introduction of television to America—as both a broadcasting medium and as a physical, wood encased unit with a screen, waiting to be adopted into the American home.

The opening of the Fair itself was hailed as a major cultural event anyway, but the presence of NBC mobile television vans, lined up at the end of the platform in the Court of Peace, further enhanced the excitement. An aerial was run up to the peak of the Federal Building, while one van acted as a transmitter, relaying the images to the main station eight miles away, atop the Empire State Building. The second van handled the pick-up. It was attached by coaxial cable with the camera on the newsreel platform, about fifty feet from the speakers at the microphones. Over 500 radio stations around the world were hooked up to the audio transmission.

The telecast opened at 12:30 p.m. with a shot of the Trylon and

Perisphere in the distance. The camera then panned across the Court of Peace for a panorama of gathering crowds, fountains and waving flags. As *The New York Times* described the scene:

"The white of the buildings and the gleaming spray of the fountains in the sun added to the effectiveness of the telecast. The parade then marched across the screen as the camera caught the various units . . . " (the strong sunlight was considered a blessing by the cameramen and technicians).

New York's Mayor Fiorello La Guardia walked directly up to the camera as he led the procession. Governor Lehman followed, but La Guardia was rated by the engineers on the mobile van as "the most telegenic man in New York." President Roosevelt's car then appeared onscreen as it entered the court. Roosevelt was later seen sitting with his wife, his mother, and other family members, before giving his speech declaring the Fair open.

Throughout the speeches the camera remained focused on the platform, providing pictures that occasionally suffered some interference as white

RCA introduces television to a curious public at the 1939 World's Fair.

streaks, believed to have been caused by switching operations. (*Variety* magazine later complained, "It was an expose, rather than a demonstration—pics flickered much too much.")

Visiting British radio officials, baffled that NBC had assigned only one camera to the event, said they would have used at least three or four camera angles for variety's sake. Then, too, they feared what might have happened if the electric eye burned out at a crucial moment. An American engineer said, "That's not our luck, but should the optic go blind, then we are licked."

Crowds at the Fair watched the televised coverage of the ceremonies on twelve television receivers with 9" x 12" screens on exhibit at the RCA building. Special screens were also installed for the public at Radio City Music Hall.

The main criticism of television viewers on the Fair grounds and at Radio City was that the camera was too far away from the speakers, causing the images to be too small. They also complained about seeing the same static shot for the entire show, unaware that the Secret Service would not permit the camera to roam around and get the lens as close to the President as the radio microphones.

Reports from receiving outposts scattered throughout a fifty-mile radius of New York indicated success. It was estimated that from 100 to 200 receivers picked up the broadcast, and that possibly 1,000 persons looked in on the pageant.

The event was acknowledged by broadcasters as the beginning of a new industry, the aim of which is to take Americans "sight-seeing by radio." Most of those involved marked down April 30, 1939, as having the same significance as that of November 2, 1910, when the radio "craze" started.

The next day, *The New York Times* reported, "Science presented television as a new deal in communication yesterday as President Roosevelt spoke in the Court of Peace at the opening of the World's Fair. For the first time a President of the United States faced a tele-camera, which for the first time took its place on the platform with a battery of newsreel cameras overlooking a historic scene."

Burke Crotty, producer in charge of the mobile units, said that much had been learned from the telecast. He confessed that the performance was far from perfect but nevertheless highly successful, considering the fact that it was the first attempt of American radio men to telecast such a vast outdoor program.

Television receivers went on sale in several New York stores the next day. Dealers prepared darkened demonstrating booths so the public might become familiar with television and with the home receivers, which sold from $200 to $1,000. An attachment to convert a radio broadcast receiver into a television instrument was priced at $200.

Regular broadcasts then began from studios at Radio City, on Wednesdays and Fridays from 8 to 9 p.m., with outdoor pick-ups at the Fair on Wednesday, Thursday, and Friday afternoons.

Variety began to review television programs as early as that June, while the staff also carefully compiled a list of television firsts, reflecting the magazine's capacity as historian of show business. Among their tallies:

The first President to be televised: F.D.R.

The first governor: Herbert H. Lehman of New York.

The first mayor: Fiorello LaGuardia.

The first name band: Fred Waring.

The first jugglers: the Three Swifts.

The first take from a Broadway show: "Mexicana."

The first fencer: Nadi.

The first midgets: Paul Remos & His Toy Boys.

The first magician: Robert Reinhart

The first tap dancer: Ann Miller.

The first harpist: Margaret Brill.

The first Negro team: Buck & Bubbles.

The first ventriloquist: Bob Neelor.

The first comic drunks: Fran (Fritz) and Jean Huber.

The first skaters and skiers: the Sun Valley Show.

The first hillbilly act: Judy Canova.

The first composer: Richard Rodgers.

The first King and Queen: George and Elizabeth.

In addition, the first fashion show on TV took place in May, broadcast from the Ritz-Carlton Hotel in New York.

Before long, however, the outbreak of war in Europe set television's progress back sharply, on both sides of the Atlantic. Upon Germany's declaration of war on September 1, 1939, Britain immediately shut down BBC television broadcasts.

As the BBC lamented in its annual year-end review, "The end came so abruptly that there was not even time for an 'au revoir' to viewers. Nor was it expedient at that time to give reasons in the press or elsewhere. How harsh this decision must have seemed to those who had just bought receivers can easily be imagined . . . Let it now be said that television closed down not because of the cost and shortage of staff, nor to difficulties with artists and transport, formidable as such obstacles would certainly have becomes, but for defence reasons."

The irony of the sudden halt in TV transmissions was not lost on the broadcasting service. "Television would, of course, have been the ideal 'black-out' entertainment. It is sad to think of the thousands of receivers now standing idle, of their disappointed viewers, and of the many skilled research and other workers in the television field diverted from their tasks . . . The brightness of the outlook for British television in the summer heightened the general sense of disappointment at its unavoidable discontinuance when war came."

America's entry into World War II in December of 1941 caused technological advances in television development here to cease for the duration. While there was not a total television shutdown, in 1942 the FCC did reduce its required number of on-air hours at licensed stations from fifteen

Baird's business partner, Oliver Hutchinson, in the first-known photo of a televised moving image.

hours per week to four hours. Only about a half-dozen stations in the country remained on the air (mostly devoted to airing war updates and civil defense content). The manufacturing of television equipment was suspended until the end of the war in August of 1945, as the research and development of television technology and manufacturing became dedicated to the war effort, especially in disciplines such as radar and communications.

But even before the war's official end, new TV programming slowly began to appear, and the sales of sets slowly increased. And, even during this period of stalled progress among manufacturers, technicians, and program producers, it was becoming evident that television would inevitably demand an enormous amount of material to broadcast.

In 1944, Thomas Hutchinson, Production Director of RKO-Television Corporation, expressed his concern over the expected need to fill television screens with enough programming:

> In the years ahead of us, I believe that the program builders of America are going to find television an insatiable monster that will devour in its stride the work and brains of thousands of men and women. Just imagine eight hours of programs a day on four competing networks. That's 11,680 hours of visual programs a

year. In 1943 the entire motion picture industry put out less than 600 hours of visual entertainment. This means that television is going to absorb the equivalent of twenty times the output of the present motion picture industry. And it's going to take the combined efforts of the network, the motion picture industry, advertising agencies and individual producers to begin to meet the future demands for television programs. It's a bright future and one we ought to get started on.

In the immediate post-war years, most new television programs were still not much more than one-shot experiments. All manner of drama, variety, audience participation, and other program formats were presented, often just for a few broadcasts, as creative and production personnel studied what worked and what didn't.

By the end of 1946, about 50,000 homes across the United States had television. The FCC's order for each broadcaster to supply twenty-eight hours of programming a week was postponed for another two years. The first full-time network schedule filled out in 1948, which also happened to be the year Milton Berle launched his landmark variety show, causing TV sales to skyrocket. By early 1949, TV sets in the U.S. passed the one million mark, and three million more would be sold that year. Only ten years later, there were an estimated 50 million sets in use.

A few words about the DuMont Network

Before we turn to examining the history of television's "Creative Firsts," let's take a brief look at one particular network that figures prominently on these pages.

If you've never heard of the DuMont Network, don't fret. You're not alone. It hasn't existed since 1956, but it was a major entity in the earliest days of network television.

Before the outbreak of World War II, Allen DuMont led his DuMont laboratories in Passaic, New Jersey, as the manufacturer of an improved TV picture tube, surpassing those made by RCA. He also owned one TV station in New York, W3XWT (later WABD—his initials), and one in Pittsburgh, WDTV. In 1938, Paramount Pictures bought partial ownership in DuMont (which actually inhibited the network's growth rather than helping it).

During the war, while most fledgling TV stations went dark, DuMont continued to grow, receiving its commercial license for WABD on June 28, 1942. By late 1945, it was being lauded for its swift progress in programming and development. *Televisor* magazine proclaimed, "Television programs over WABD-DuMont, New York, have probably been more extensive and varied during the past couple of years than those of any other station in the country."

In 1946, DuMont became the fourth TV network, alongside CBS, NBC, and ABC. Unlike its competitors, however, it did not already have an established network of radio stations and a line-up of sponsors on which to build a potentially nationwide web of TV affiliates. This proved to be the most damaging factor leading to DuMont's ultimate demise. Production-wise, the network moved into the basement of Wanamaker's department store in Herald Square, in Manhattan, where the budgets for DuMont productions were notoriously skimpy.

However, several now-classic, even historic, programs were born under the DuMont name, including *The Jackie Gleason Show* and *Cavalcade of Stars,* which morphed into *Your Show of Shows,* starring Sid Caesar. DuMont also gave American network television its first children's program, first police drama, first soap opera, first science fiction show, and first telethon. In addition, DuMont was the only network to provide gavel-to-gavel coverage of the notorious 1954 Army-McCarthy hearings, during which Senator Joseph McCarthy conducted his infamous witch hunt of alleged Communist sympathizers in the military.

However, DuMont simply couldn't maintain its competition with the other networks, and folded in 1956.

CHAPTER 2
THE CREATIVE FIRSTS

The first drama ever performed on TV

On September 11, 1928, *The Queen's Messenger,* a play written by J. Hartley Manners and first performed in 1899, became the first drama of *any* kind performed on a television broadcast. It was televised from General Electric's experimental station W2XB (WGY) in Schenectady, and has been described as "one of those high-society, European-setting melodramas, with fancy cigarettes, switched suitcases, and heroic sacrifices, which were so popular on the stage at the turn of the century." The historic performance starred Izettea Jewell, a retired stage actress, and Maurice Randall, a radio actor at WGY. The broadcast's producer/director, Mortimer Stewart, had presented many radio plays from WGY and NBC's New York station.

There were actually three cameras, or transmitters, present in the studio—one camera for shots of Jewell, another for Randall, and a third for shots of hands manipulating various props, such as cigarettes, pistols, and knives. For this arrangement, it was necessary for each actor to have an assistant. The hands of Joyce Evans Rector and production assistant William Toneski were used in close-ups, handling the props. There was also a radio microphone in front of each actor.

The crude equipment of the time still enabled director Stewart to fade the actors in and out of each scene, as is done on film. Stewart stood in front of a special receiving set, so that he could see the images as they appeared on the television receiver, and check them with the voices.

The crowded set of *The Queen's Messenger.*

In 1931, Toneski wrote a detailed account of the production. "From the very beginning we ran into difficulties," he revealed. "Because of their newness, the photoelectric cells, the 'scanning machines' or 'cameras' and the 'monitor' were merely 'this box' or 'that box.' Gradually, by the process of elimination, we finally reached a point where the same name was used by all the people in the studio . . ."

Then an unexpected distraction challenged the actors: "Difficulty was also experienced when the actors were placed before the flickering light produced by the rotation of the scanning disc. Not only was the flicker distracting at first, but also slight headaches resulted; and the actors, though equally experienced before microphone and footlights, found it difficult to remember their lines."

Toneski further explained that each actor also had to keep his or her head in focus, because the lens of the scanning machine concentrated the beam of light at a certain distance from the camera. The actors had to keep themselves from making any sudden movements beyond certain physical parameters, such as moving forward or backwards too far beyond the focal range. New make-up had to be devised as well, to keep facial features from washing out under the strong lights. The play was broadcast at 1:30 in the afternoon, the regular time when the lab aired its experimental transmissions, and was repeated at 11:30 that evening.

The TV signal traveled only a few miles, to be received by a grand total of four receiving sets, each with a small screen measuring only about 3 x 3 inches. The images were reported to be blurred and confused at times, and were not always holding the center of the screens. As described by Russell B. Porter in *The New York Times* the next day, the pictures "were sometimes hard on the eyes because of the way in which they flickered . . . The effect was the same as listening to a play by radio, as every radio fan can do, except that in addition one could see moving pictures of the actors as they spoke their lines and did their stage 'business' . . . "

The program was transmitted both by wire connections as well as over-the-air, and "those who saw it both ways said that the actual broadcasting gave even better results than the wire connections."

Despite technical shortcomings, the broadcast was such a major event it was given a front-page headline in *The New York Times*. "For the first time in history," wrote Porter, "a dramatic performance was broadcast simultaneously by radio and television . . . While the actors went through their parts in a locked studio room, the audience saw and heard them over a synchronized radio-television receiving set in another room in the same building. Their appearance and voices, translated into electronic impulses, were carried by land wire to transmitting station WGY, four miles away, were broadcast from there, and were picked up again at the place of origin."

Porter then speculated on television's potential. "Great as has been the success of the talking movies, they may easily be outdone by radio-television if the technical difficulties are overcome, for then radio-television will bring both the words and scenes of dramatic and musical performances, besides public events and athletic contests, into the home as well as into theatres."

The Queen's Messenger was the first dramatic work to be performed on television, but the first original play written *specifically* for TV was *The Love Nest*, written by and co-starring a young Eddie Albert. It was performed in NBC Studio 3H in Rockefeller Center on September 21, 1936. Albert was

Eddie Albert and Grace Brandt perform in *The Love Nest*.

still a struggling actor at the time, doing a nightclub act in New York with Grace Bradt, when a talent scout at NBC saw their act and had them meet with executives. The execs asked Albert to come up with something for a television test shoot for one of the network's big sponsors, General Foods. Albert wrote a playlet called *The Love Nest*, basically a lengthy commercial for various General Foods products, in which he and Bradt portrayed a couple having dinner at home. The September 21 "broadcast" from NBC Studio 3H in Rockefeller Center, was in fact not seen outside the confines of the RCA building, but rather studied by only a few dozen technicians and advertising executives. However, it is considered to be the first original play of any kind to be written specifically for TV.

The first regularly scheduled network drama series

In April 1945, NBC aired the premiere episode of the weekly drama series *NBC Television Theater,* which favored productions adapted from the stage, rather than from radio.

Kraft became the program's sponsor two years later, when the program was re-launched as *Kraft Television Theatre* on May 7, 1947. It holds a special place in television history not only as the first weekly dramatic series, but also as the first dramatic anthology program. And, considering it began its run so early in the history of network broadcasting, it created a standard of excellence in its dramatic presentations that subsequent network anthology programs sought to emulate.

Closely following *Kraft Television Theatre* were almost a dozen anthology programs that enjoyed long runs throughout the 1950s, including *Philco TV Playhouse, Studio One, Robert Montgomery Presents,* and *Lux Video Theatre.*

Kraft Television Theatre had been going strong for seven years—and without even taking a summer hiatus each year—when, on October 15, 1955, a second *Kraft Theatre* installment was launched and aired on Thursday nights, making a total of 104 hours of live televised plays a year. *TV Guide* noted that in so doing, "a TV show has become the biggest single theatrical enterprise in history . . . viewers will be able to see on the two Kraft shows alone almost two-thirds as many hours of drama each year as are staged by all producers on Broadway."

Script editors Ed Rice and Arthur Heineman chose one script out of ten each week to produce on the air, so in order to televise 104 plays, they needed to read through over a thousand scripts yearly. The program aired its final episode on October 1, 1958.

The first prime time network sitcom

The first original sitcom to air in prime time on a network was *Mary Kay and Johnny,* premiering in November 1947 on the DuMont network, and starring real-life married couple Mary Kay and Johnny Stearns.

The two were up-and-coming young stage actors in New York when they met and fell in love in 1946. Both had been appearing in Broadway productions together and separately when, in 1947, Mary Kay was made aware of an on-camera television job opening at the DuMont studios, located in Wanamaker's department store in lower Manhattan. The 15-minute weekly program, *Jay Jay Junior Dresses*, was a simple fashion show sponsored by dress manufacturer Jay Jossel. Mary Kay's job was to model a few dresses per program, speak to the viewers about the fine points of each outfit, and introduce brief film clips that would run as she made a quick change from one dress to another.

Before long, Jossel realized that most of the televisions in New York were found in bars, where most viewers were male, and thus unlikely to appreciate a TV fashion show for women. He was about to give up his sponsorship of the time slot when Johnny asked if he could use the air time to try something different: a radio-style domestic comedy for television, starring himself and Mary Kay. Jossel agreed, with one proviso. A friend of his manufactured cosmetic compacts with a mirror attached. If Mary Kay pitched the product at the end of the time slot, and sold 200 compacts, the duo could take over the time slot to produce Johnny's domestic comedy.

Johnny wrote a 15-minute script based on his and Mary Kay's real life, and, on November 18, *Mary Kay and Johnny* debuted at 9:00 p.m. (its first of many time slots). As agreed, Mary Kay concluded the program with the sales pitch for the compacts. Within days, Jossel reported nearly 9,000 responses to the program (and a good deal more than 200 compacts sold), and presented a contract to the couple to continue their program.

Johnny was not a professional writer and never claimed to be, but the scripts came to him easily, since they were based on his and Mary Kay's personal experiences as a young married couple. He was simply following the old adage for writers, "*write what you know best.*"

"If we portray ourselves," he explained decades later in an interview for the Television Academy's video archives, "some people may not like us, but they wouldn't like us if they knew us. But if we're totally ourselves, people can't say they don't believe us. And so for that reason, we wrote very close to home, obviously dramatizing and going for gags and comedy, but keeping it on things that actually happened to us."

The show took place in the couple's Greenwich Village apartment. Mary Kay's character was perky, enthusiastic, but a bit of a screwball, while strait-laced bank teller Johnny found himself spending much of his time getting her out of various minor crises. "Because of Mary Kay's big, generous heart, she would create a situation that would put me in a real bind, but by the time [the episode] was over, she either intentionally or unintentionally would get me out of the bind."

The production was simple and low-budget—typical not only for that early period of TV history, but also for DuMont's infamous shoestring operation. A three-sided living room set was provided, furnished with pieces from Wanamaker's store displays. Johnny was writer, producer, and de-facto director. When he was on camera, a sole technical director sat in the control booth, punching the buttons to switch shots between the two studio cameras.

After the program had been on for half a year, Mary Kay became pregnant with the couple's first child, and Johnny simply wrote that into the

Mary Kay & Johnny

scripts, making her the first pregnant female character on a TV series (they were also the first couple to share a bed on TV). In the early autumn of 1948, Whitehall Pharmaceuticals decided it wanted to sponsor a domestic comedy, and hired Mary Kay and Johnny to do a half-hour version of the show for NBC. This meant shooting the show at the studios in Rockefeller Center, which afforded the program higher production values.

In October, *Variety* magazine offered its take on the show. "Much of the show's charm is traceable directly to the femme half of the team, who displayed a pleasant personality that prototyped the average conception of a young American housefrau [sic]. . . [The] storyline picked them up with Mary Kay making plans for her first baby, which is due in a couple months, and her difficulties in buying the right baby carriage. It was that simple, but also that good. Whether the gal is actually going to have a baby wasn't made clear, but it would be a neat idea for the series . . . "

Christopher was born on December 19, 1948, but even his arrival didn't hinder the Stearns's commitment to the show. That night's episode was shot thirty minutes after Christopher's birth, and showed an 'expectant' Johnny Stearns pacing the waiting room floor. Mary Kay missed only two programs for the birth, and Christopher even appeared briefly on his first episode when he was only ten days old.

Continuing the program at NBC's studios at Rockefeller center had its advantages, including a bigger budget and more impressive sets. The studio crew was bigger, and there were three cameras following the action instead of two. Bud Yorkin, future creative partner with Norman Lear, was a cameraman on the show, and future Emmy-winning director Paul Bogart (who also later worked with Lear on *All in the Family*) was the studio floor manager. In addition, some of the Stearns's young actor friends at the time appeared on the show, including Jack Gilford as the neighborhood grocer, James Whitmore as a cop, and Howard Morris, soon to be one of Sid Caesar's TV comic foils.

But the half-hour shows proved more challenging for Johnny to write. He often tried to bring new writers to help share the load, but none of them managed to capture the couple's real life situations satisfactorily. The program moved to CBS for part of 1949, but Johnny's goal of finding a writing staff he could be comfortable with still eluded him. Finally, that summer, the show returned to NBC, and to its original 15-minute running time. But, after a jumping back to a 30-minute format yet again, Johnny decided that he was too exhausted to continue, and the program ended its run in March of 1950. Still, he and Mary Kay appreciated being recognized on the street, and were grateful for the fan mail, but, as Johnny insisted, "We purposely did not want to be celebrities."

Johnny continued a busy career as a producer and director, while Mary Kay continued work on Broadway and occasional television. They were married for fifty-five years until Johnny's death in 2001.

The first several months of *Mary Kay and Johnny* episodes were not recorded via kinescopes, and, according to Johnny, only special episodes were preserved at first, due to budget considerations. But, while more episodes were recorded for later airing on the West Coast, their ultimate fate was the same as that of most DuMont programs: In 1975, a vast majority of all DuMont program kinescopes on 16 mm film were disposed of in New York's East River, to make room in the warehouse of the network's successor, Metromedia. It's been reported that only a single episode of *Mary Kay and Johnny* exists today.

Keeping in mind that *Mary Kay and Johnny* was created as a 15-minute show, the 1949 syndicated comedy *Jackson and Jill* was the first sitcom to be created as a half-hour show. It ran for four years.

The first series to crossover from radio to television

By the late 1940s, radio had enjoyed a quarter-century as a hugely popular and influential presence in virtually every American home. News and entertainment programs kept Americans connected through the Great Depression and World War II. The emergence of television, then, brought with it a great mix of excitement, trepidation, and curiosity among those involved in entertainment as well as the general public.

It may seem, with television's growing presence in those immediate post-war years, that a radio program could either remain a radio program, or make a total transition to television, but couldn't possibly do both at the same time. However, in the late 1940s, there were a fair number of programs that did just that. Modifications were made to broadcast studios, in an effort to make programs visually appealing for television.

We the People was the first program to do this, on June 1, 1948. In October, *America's Town Meeting* did likewise. Not only were both programs considered the easiest to welcome TV cameras into their studios, but the in-studio audience was essential for each show. Other radio programs that were also deemed the least complicated to simulcast on TV included game show *Break the Bank* (with host Bert Parks), *Arthur Godfrey's Talent Scouts*, and *The Chesterfield Supper Club* (hosted by Perry Como), all of which debuted on television before the end of 1948, while also maintaining their status as radio programs.

In January 1949, *The Goldbergs*, a radio favorite since 1929, aired its first episode for television on CBS, becoming the first *scripted* series to make the full transition from radio to TV. This gentle, popular comedy about the life of a Jewish family in a New York tenement, was created by and starred Gertrude Berg, who, between the radio and TV versions, wrote over 10,000 scripts single-handedly.

At that same time, NBC president Niles Trammell expressed his desire for a regular TV series with recurring characters and a familiar setting, with which viewers could get comfortable over time. Trammel reasoned that "the five times a week continued story should be effective and relatively economical on television. The characters would be used with very little change in scenery. There also would appear to be a place in television for the one time a week continuing story, utilizing the same characters... these are program formats which appear to be good television material."

In that light, *Television* magazine expressed its appreciation of *The Goldbergs*:

CBS has come forth with such a format in *The Goldberg's*. This
old AM show has succeeded like very few television programs
in projecting itself so completely into the family circle. There has

been a lot of talk in television for many years about what is "good television." There can be no doubt that the Goldberg family is "good television." In fact the Goldberg's *are* television.

Mrs. Berg writes a script that has great pictorial content. It is at once intimate, sincere, and appealing. For many years she has exhibited ability to derive much from the little things of life which, though often obvious, are never tiresome when her characters dramatize them. Much credit is due to CBS's Worthington Miner for his complete understanding of the medium and adapting *The Goldberg's* to television.

A year before the TV series debuted, Berg also wrote *Me and Molly,* a stage version of *The Goldbergs,* which ran on Broadway for 156 performances. And, in 1951, a film version, titled simply *Molly,* was released, making *The Goldbergs* the only sitcom in history to have been produced on radio, television, stage, and film. As Berg explained her ability to write so easily for all media, "This may sound odd, but to me writing *The Goldbergs* for television is almost exactly the same as doing the job for radio or the stage . . . I do not mean to imply that presenting *The Goldbergs* on television is not hard work. We would not be rehearsing 33 hours every week for our half-hour show if it were easy. But the point I make is that television called for no important change in writing and even in acting technique from the radio version."

But even television's warm welcome for the fictional Jewish Bronx family was not without shades of trepidation, due to their ethnicity. Just a few months after the TV program's debut, a commentary in *Television* magazine pointed to an episode in which the Goldbergs attended a Park Avenue pyramid party. "They were looked down upon, pictured as noisy and, to an extent, objectionable to the hostess and her friends of the Park Ave. set. It made for uneasy viewing for the TV audience.

"It's our feeling that as long as the Goldbergs stay in their own element in the Bronx, the TV audience gets the benefit of a warm and fascinating segment of American life. Certainly there could be no objection here. But when

Gertrude Berg as Molly Goldberg keeping tabs on her neighbors,
joined by Eli Mintz as Uncle Dave.
Note the sponsor's Sanka coffee tin serving as a flower pot.

a contrast is made with another pattern of that same American life the results can be confusing, and a hindrance to the cause of better understanding."

When co-star Philip Loeb was blacklisted for suspected Communist activities, CBS and the program's sponsor, General Foods, pressured Berg to fire him. She refused, so CBS dropped the show in June of 1951, after which it appeared on NBC, which also pressured Berg to dismiss Loeb. She reluctantly gave in (but secretly continued paying his salary (Loeb committed suicide in 1955). This NBC version of the show aired in a twice-weekly, 15-minute format.

The program moved yet again, to the DuMont Network, in 1954, where it reverted back to a weekly half-hour show. Finally, a syndicated filmed version, with the Goldbergs moving to a modest home in the suburbs, aired on local stations until 1956.

Jewish lead or recurring characters disappeared from network entertainment programs until 1970, when Rhoda Morgenstern appeared as a supporting character on *The Mary Tyler Moore Show*. And, of course, Rhoda continued as the lead in the spin-off series *Rhoda* in 1974.

The migration from radio to television

As it became obvious that television was about to become an unstoppable force in the entertainment industry, it also became apparent to industry insiders that even seasoned radio veterans—be they writers, actors, or production technicians—needed to learn the ropes for working in television, if they were to have any chance of making a successful transition. And, with the FCC demanding a 28-hour schedule per network by 1946 (later postponed to 1948), the need for new material created specifically for the tube was only going to grow. To that end, the Radio Writers' Guild took a proactive way of addressing the issue of teaching radio writers how to write television scripts. The Guild essentially sent its members back to school, in the form of seminars headed by Norman Rosen, a television director of the J. Walter Thompson Advertising Agency. As *Television* magazine explained at the time, "The writers group, which is made up of radio's biggest names, is planning to take members behind the scenes of live productions. They will be shown the technical and creative sides of tele-production. Station and agency tele-personnel have signified willingness to cooperate."

Group members wrote experimental scripts as part of the curriculum, the best of which were paid for and produced over local stations.

Engineering and technical unions had been providing the same educational courses for their members, but, "this action by the Guild is the first step in the direction of getting creative-production personnel on the know-how ball. Open only to members in good standing, this promises to be one of the most valuable of the Radio Writer's Guild's undertakings."

While this was all well and good, there was some question as to whether or not radio was really the best place to turn for potential television performers. After all, even experienced radio stars—dramatic actors, comedians, and others—were accustomed to reading their lines from scripts while standing in front of stationary microphones. There was no need to memorize anything, or to rehearse movement, or "blocking," around a set while reciting dialogue. The implications of performing a scene in front of cameras that could catch each and every movement and facial expression didn't seem to occur to many radio stars as they felt themselves drawn to television.

As Ralph Austrian, Vice-President of the RKO Television Corporation, posed the question in 1945, "The radio actor should ask himself, 'Am I an actor or just a reader of lines?' Can I memorize half a hundred sides a week? . . . How do I look before the camera—am I photogenic, or am I suitable for character parts? If he can only muster negatives to the above questions he has cause for worry."

With television enjoying a major burst of popularity in 1948, it looked certain that radio, as it had been known for the previous two decades, was beginning to lose its life force to the flickering screen. Many individual performers began testing the television waters as the first non-scripted radio programs, such as *The Original Amateur Hour,* and the news/public affairs program *Meet the Press,* made a clean break and successfully left radio behind altogether, to make a complete transition to television.

The same year that *The Goldbergs* made the move to television, other scripted radio shows, including the sitcoms *The Aldrich Family* and *The Life of Riley,* also made the crossover. Both premiered on NBC in October of 1949.

The first radio drama to make the transition to television, *Suspense,* was a highly-honored dramatic anthology dating to 1942. While continuing on radio, the television version premiered on CBS on March 1, 1949. The program aired live, with many stories starring some of the finest actors of the time.

But the entertainment industry's transition from radio to television was just as challenging for some of the top radio comedians of the day as it was for dramatic radio actors. Fred Allen, one of radio's most popular comedians, was famous for his disdain for television. "Berle isn't doing anything for television," he said in 1949. "He's photographing a vaudeville act. That's what they're all doing. Even *The Goldbergs*, which has been so well received, gets tiresome after you see it four or five times. You know what the uncle is going to do and you know what the kids are going to do. The trouble with television is it's too graphic. In radio, even a moron could visualize things his way; an intelligent man, his way. It was a custom-made suit. Television is a ready-made suit. Everyone has to wear the same one . . . "

Allen went on to reveal what he considered to be a source of some anxiety for all radio comedians. "We all have a great problem—Benny, Hope, all of us. We don't know how to duplicate our success in radio. We found out how to cope with radio and, and after seventeen years, you know pretty well what effect you're achieving. But those things won't work in television. Jack Benny's sound effects, Fibber's closet—they won't be funny in television. We don't know what will be funny or even whether our looks are acceptable." Of course, Allen was proven wrong about his comedy contemporaries, the great majority of whom fared extremely well on television. But it was Allen himself who became infamous for failing to find a suitable format for his talents on TV.

The first sitcom to use a laugh track

The Hank McCune Show, a sitcom which first aired locally in Los Angeles in late 1949, lasted on the NBC network for all of three months, from September to December of 1950. McCune played a fictional and disaster-prone version of himself, with help from stalwart comic actors Larry Keating (*The Burns & Allen Show*) and Arthur Q. Bryan (the original voice of Elmer Fudd). *Variety* magazine, in reviewing the show, made special mention of the laugh track, noting that the sitcom "has an innovation in a sound track that contains audience laughter. Although the show is lensed on film without a studio audience, there are chuckles and yocks dubbed in. Whether this induces a jovial mood in home viewers is still to be determined, but the practice may have unlimited possibilities, if it's spared to include canned peals of hilarity, thunderous ovations and gasps of sympathy."

Those who have seen episodes of *The Life of Riley* from its initial 1949 season, starring Jackie Gleason, will notice a laugh track on that show as well (Gleason's first and only season on the show was not successful; he was replaced by William Bendix when the series was revived in 1953). That laughter, however, was not part of the original production. Producer Irving Brecher was forced to work with such a limited budget, he could not afford the inclusion of a laugh track at the time. He added the laughter decades later, upon the re-issue of the series for syndication.

Ironically, going back before television to the early days of radio, the sound of *any* audience laughter following a joke on a comedy program was, throughout the 1920s, considered by most radio executives to be too distracting, even confusing, to listeners at home. Consequently, the infamous "glass curtain" was installed in recording auditoriums. Audiences were invited to sit and watch on-air performances, but were sternly discouraged from laughing out loud. The glass curtain served as a physical and aural barrier to ensure quiet during the programs. This did not deter comedians such as Eddie Cantor and Ed Wynn, who, on their own programs in the early 1930s, relied a great deal on visual comedy, and often included sight gags on their shows for the studio audience's enjoyment. Of course, the source of their laughter was lost on radio listeners. John Carlisle, Director of Programming for CBS, complained, "To sit by a radio receiver and hear laughter without knowing what provoked it is extremely annoying. So annoying, in fact, that some comedians would do better to work without a studio audience." But Carlisle soon lost the philosophical argument, and the glass curtain was forever banished from radio.

As for television, from *The Hank McClune Show* onward, the use of the laugh track has had a sort of now-you-hear-it, now-you-don't history. Its use actually dates back to the twilight of radio's Golden Era in the late 1940s. The use of the laugh machine, invented by audio engineer Charley Douglas for Bing Crosby's program, was carried over to television not only on *The Hank McClune Show*, but on all single-camera—and sometimes studio—sitcoms throughout the 1950s and 1960s (sitcoms like *The Donna Reed Show* and *Father Knows Best* went one better, by adding an *applause* track for the final fade-out shot of each episode). In some cases, especially for sitcoms that incorporated special effects and/or tricky film editing (*Mr. Ed, I Dream of Jeannie, Bewitched*), filming before a studio audience obviously wasn't practical, but hearing disembodied laughter throughout each episode was still considered a necessity.

Even some drama series in the 1950s felt compelled to add a laugh track to the occasional humorous episode. *The Millionaire*, for example, was basically a dramatic program, but a first- season comedic episode in 1955, "The Harvey Blake Story," included a laugh track (as if the viewing audience at home wouldn't recognize it as a comedy without the help of canned laughter). Likewise, *The Twilight Zone* occasionally presented episodes lighter in tone than its usual menu of sci-fi/paranormal/horror, and added a laugh track to only one of those humorous installments, "Cavender Is Coming," starring Carol Burnett and Jesse White. Producer Buck Houghton once explained that the addition of a laugh track to the episode "was CBS's idea, because they were in a pilot mood and they wanted to get a Jesse White thing going. I refused to go to the dubbing session with the canned laughter man there. I thought it was a dreadful idea." On the bright side, the episode has also been syndicated with the laugh track removed.

While the use of the laugh track on sitcoms reached a peak in the mid-1960s, programs such as *The Dick van Dyke Show, The Lucy Show, The Mothers-In-Law,* and *He and She* were all filmed before live audiences.

As the decade came to a close, a few single-camera sitcoms—*Julia, The Bill Cosby Show, Room 222*—detoured from the more traditional route by not including a laugh track at all. It could be argued, however, that the actual comedy content in those shows was so light as to call into question whether they were really comedies at all.

The live audience gradually came back into favor more strongly in the early 1970s, with *The Mary Tyler Moore Show,* as well as all other MTM productions, and with Norman Lear's sitcoms, beginning with *All in the Family* (Lear's soap opera satire *Mary Hartman, Mary Hartman,* was the only one of his programs taped without an audience, naturally).

The TV version of Neil Simon's *The Odd Couple,* premiered in September 1970, and produced its first season with a laugh track, but stars Tony Randall and Jack Klugman soon expressed their unhappiness, claiming that their timing would be much improved with a studio audience present (one episode that aired without a laugh track didn't seem to feel right, either). So, beginning with the series' second season, the show was filmed before a studio audience.

But even with the return of studio audiences in sitcoms, the laugh track never totally disappeared from television. In 1972, *M*A*S*H,* based on the 1970 film, began its eleven-year run as a sitcom, using a laugh track—again at the insistence of CBS—in all but a handful of episodes. However, the series' producers were adamant that the laugh track be omitted from all scenes taking place in the operating room. As Alan Alda explained in 1980, "I'm not a fan of laugh tracks. They show our show in England without one, and it does fine over there. I get a number of letters every year from people who complain about the laugh track—but, interestingly, a number of them have enjoyed the show for years and think that we have just started a laugh track this season . . . I think the reason for that is that we have always kept the laugh track very low and very, very quiet, very, very low-key, as unobtrusive as we can make it. It's only there because the network, as all three networks do, considers it to be essential to a program that's mainly funny."

For the ninth and final season of *All in the Family* (before it morphed into *Archie Bunker's Place*), star Carroll O'Connor decided that he preferred taping the episodes *without* a studio audience present. His wishes were granted, although a modified use of the conventional laugh track was incorporated into those later episodes. Once each episode was shot and edited, an audience was brought into the studio, shown the episode on monitors, and their laughter and other reactions were recorded, to be added to the audio track before broadcast. O'Connor's voiceover accompanying the closing credits informed viewers: "*All in the Family* was played to a studio audience for live responses." Actually, this practice has been commonly used in British sitcoms for decades, whereby scenes filmed on location are shot ahead of time, edited, and then screened for the studio audience already present for the taping of that same episode's studio scenes. In America, this was also done in more recent years for the CBS sitcom *How I Met Your Mother*.

It was one thing for programs like *The Odd Couple* and, in its third season, *Happy Days,* to revamp themselves and replace a laugh track with a live studio audience, but the *reverse* process played out during the production of another popular 1970s sitcom, *Barney Miller.* Premiering in 1975, the show was taped before a studio audience, and usually performed on a single set, much like a play. But the series dropped the live audience in its fourth season. As Hal Linden explained in 1980, "Most of the scenes in *Barney Miller* are very small—delicate nuances of what's going on. With an audience, the tendency of actors is to reach out and make those moments overblown . . . One week the script was so late that we didn't have time to rehearse, so we skipped the audience. And the show wasn't any worse for it. So we said, 'What's the sense of having all the pressure of getting the show in shape to shoot in front of an audience?' Now we shoot it like a film, scene by scene, except we use multiple cameras. It gives us the great advantage of having time to work on a scene, to work piece by piece without the pressure of the next scene. Now we shoot in two days instead of one; it's more expensive . . . but everybody seems to think it's worth it."

The laugh track survives to this day mostly on some cable network sitcoms, especially those geared for young audiences on the Nickelodeon and Disney channels.

The first sitcom shot in front of a live audience

As the 1950s began, there were still questions among television professionals concerning just about every aspect of how television programs should or shouldn't be produced. Everyone from the top network executives to directors, audio engineers, lighting and camera operators, were taking baby steps as they developed their ideas on how to best utilize television's potential.

One of the questions at the time was whether or not television programs should even have studio audiences present during broadcasts. In 1946, RCA vice-president Alfred Goldsmith addressed the issue, and despite his half-hearted attempt to present the pros and cons equally, he was clearly against the idea. His first argument held that the public should not be invited to observe the behind-the-scenes workings of a television production, lest that destroy the same illusion that a feature film needs to draw in and captivate its audience. "In a fundamental respect," Goldsmith said, "the idea of public audiences 'behind the scenes' is entirely contrary to the traditions of the entertainment industry. These industries ... are fundamentally sellers of glamour and venders of illusion. As such, the more effectively they shatter the illusions they present, the less attractive the resulting performance. The motion picture industry ... rigidly and properly excludes the public from the stages on which the feature films of the future are under preparation." He then likened the production of a film to a magician's trick, the technique of which is never revealed to the audience. While he acknowledged how some programs, such as game and quiz shows, couldn't exist without a studio audience present, he also continued with additional reasons, both practical and philosophical, why he felt television should strive to keep studio audiences at bay.

Of course, Goldsmith's arguments didn't take hold in the case of the sitcom, which leads us to the first sitcom to be shot in front of a live audience, *I Love Lucy*. The series debuted on October 15, 1951, beginning a seven-year run.

I Love Lucy.

Lucille Ball was just coming off the successful run of the radio sitcom *My Favorite Husband,* with Richard Denning, when CBS asked her and Denning to star in a TV version of the show. Instead, she and husband Desi Arnaz decided to attempt a new TV series in which they could star together. At the time, most TV programs, including sitcoms, were produced in New York and aired live. Before the introduction of videotape, kinescopes of the programs were then physically delivered to stations elsewhere in the country for broadcast, sometimes a week after their original transmission.

As the plans for *I Love Lucy* developed, several significant decisions needed to be made, such as whether the show should be produced in New York or Los Angeles, and whether it should be shot live and preserved and distributed on kinescopes, or shot on film, to ensure better and longer lasting picture quality. As various debates of these issues took place between the production team, CBS, and sponsor Phillip Morris, Arnaz and producer Jess Oppenheimer decided that Ball would work better in front of an audience.

It was also decided that the show would be produced in Los Angeles and on film, but there were no film studios available that could safely accommodate a studio audience. After an extensive search, Arnaz and Oppenheimer finally found General Service Studios in Hollywood, which agreed to make the necessary renovations to allow for an audience.

Production began with three 35mm cameras capturing the action of each episode (thus cutting down on the number of necessary re-takes), and a live studio audience present to laugh at Lucy's antics as they happened. The standard method of producing multi-camera sitcoms was then pretty much set for decades to come.

But just to clear up a few common misconceptions: *I Love Lucy* was *not* the first TV program to be filmed in front of a live audience; that distinction goes to the game show *You Bet Your Life,* hosted by Groucho Marx, which crossed over from radio to TV, premiering on the tube in 1950 (more about that later). And, *I Love Lucy* was not even the first sitcom to use a multi-camera format. The syndicated sitcom *Jackson and Jill* did so when it first aired in 1949, albeit that production used 16mm film, as opposed to the superior 35mm later used for *I Love Lucy.*

The first science fiction show on TV

Captain Video and his Video Rangers, a children's space adventure program set in the future, premiered on the DuMont network on June 27, 1949, thus becoming the first sci-fi show of any kind on television. Captain Video (played in the first season by Richard Coogan, and thereafter by Al Hodge) was, according to the opening voice-over, a "electronic wizard, master of time and space, and Guardian of the Safety of the World." He led a network of his Video Rangers to battle villains bent on conquering Earth, and devised and employed an arsenal of space-age weapons to ensure his success.

A good deal of the action took place at the Video Rangers' headquarters, adorned with flashing bulbs, control panels, dials, and other bells and whistles. The limited production budget for the show—as well as that of all DuMont programs—was the stuff of legend in the TV industry. The painted interior sets looked flimsy, and the budget for props was limited to twenty-five dollars a week. However, *Captain Video's* razzle-dazzle impressed some reviewers. *The New York Times* reported that "it boasts enough fancy gadgets to bewilder the adult and fascinate the youngster," but hastened to add that "*Captain Video* is a triumph of carpentry and wiring rather than writing . . . It is from the use of setting, props and special effects that Captain Video derives its appeal, and each testifies to the imagination of M.C. Brock, the program's creator."

Indeed, the writing was not held in especially high esteem, even by the cast. "We have to run through it to get the laughs out," Coogan confessed at the time. "The lines are so corny that we always break up in rehearsal."

The show quickly inspired similar space-adventure programs designed for a young audience, such as *Space Patrol* and *Tom Corbett, Space Cadet.* But *Captain Video* achieved the kind of popularity that prompted other TV genres to pay it due recognition, even if it was satirical in nature. In the first of the "Classic 39" episodes of the half-hour version of *The Honeymooners* in 1955, Ralph Kramden's neighbor Ed Norton reveals his obsession with *Captain Video* as the two friends attempt to share a single TV set between them.

Captain Video ended its run in April of 1955.

Science fiction on television matured throughout the 1950s and into the 1960s, often straying from the rocket ship/silver jump suit motif to more adult-minded paranormal themes, presenting stories in which the everyday lives of normal people are disrupted by the paranormal and unexplained phenomena. *The Twilight Zone* took the lead in this direction with its debut in 1959, followed later that same year by *One Step Beyond*. *Thriller,* hosted by Boris Karloff, joined their ranks in 1960, while *The Outer Limits* took to the airwaves in 1963, with its own ample offerings of freakish monsters, robots, and aliens.

In Britain, an afternoon sci-fi program aimed at youngsters made its debut in 1963 as well. *Dr. Who* had little to indicate at the time that it would gain a cult following, then grow beyond cult status and become one of the most popular and longest running sci-fi programs in the world (even with changes in lead actors playing the title character).

With the premiere of *Star Trek* in 1966, the sci-fi genre on American TV took a major leap in storytelling style. Creator Gene Roddenberry had pitched his idea to NBC executives as "*Wagon Train* to the stars," and then proceeded to create memorable characters and stories spanning the galaxies, sometimes offering space-age parables based on social issues, prejudices, and moral dilemmas so common on Earth.

Meanwhile, film producer-director Irwin Allen got busy bringing a slew of his own sci-fi series to the screen. Beginning in 1964, *Voyage to the Bottom of the Sea* (based on Allen's 1961 film), *Lost in Space, The Time Tunnel,* and *Land of the Giants* all premiered within four years of each other, and all tended to be more reliant on elaborate sets and special effects than on clever scripts and convincing acting.

The 1970s saw *The Six-Million Dollar Man* and its spinoff, *The Bionic Woman,* score huge ratings for ABC, and a sci-fi highlight in the 1980s came in the form of the miniseries *V,* its sequel, and then a weekly series.

The science fiction genre on TV got a big boost with the creation of cable's Sci-Fi Channel, which launched on September 24, 1992, highlighted with its broadcast of *Star Wars*. As it gained a following by airing reruns of sci-fi and horror series and feature films, it also entered the realm of original productions.

On the broadcast networks, sci-fi storytelling continued in the late 1990s with the Chris Carter series *The X-Files* and *Millennium*. Joss Whedon also contributed several series to the genre that deftly combined elements of sci-fi, horror, and humor with *Buffy the Vampire Slayer*, *Tru Calling*, *Dollhouse*, and *Firefly*.

The first TV western

For all practical purposes, the TV western is a genre that has become extinct. The last weekly prime time network series to take place in the Old West was NBC's *Dr. Quinn, Medicine Woman*, starring Jane Seymour, which began its run in January 1993, and ended in May 1998.

But once upon a time—in the late 1950s to be exact—westerns were multiplying on television like rabbits, much to the chagrin of many critics, but to the delight of manufacturers and advertisers of toy rifles and cowboy hats.

The first western series on television, *Hopalong Cassidy*, was not created specifically for TV, but was a successful series of "B" Westerns popular with the Saturday matinee crowd in the early 1940s. The series starred William Boyd, who first appeared on film as Hopalong in 1935, and who later had the foresight to buy the television rights to the film series for $350,000. They first aired in New York as early as 1945, but Boyd later added narration and new scenes to the originals for regular broadcasts. On August 7, 1948, KTLA in Los Angeles first broadcast the revised versions of the films. Boyd then continued to star in newly-produced episodes, which aired on the NBC network beginning in April of 1950. The series ceased production in December of 1951, but reruns continued in syndication.

As mentioned earlier, *The Lone Ranger* was created by George Trendle and Fran Striker for radio in 1933, and became a nationwide favorite. A film serial followed, and the radio version later made the transition to television on ABC, with its premiere episode airing on September 15, 1949. The series was filmed especially for television, rather than re-editing installments from the movie serial. By the following year, it became the ABC network's highest rated series, and ran for eight seasons (John Hart replaced Moore from 1952 to 1954, when Moore refused to continue during a contract dispute. Jay Silverheels played Tonto for the entire run).

Good natured—and sometimes singing—cowboys like Gene Autry and Roy Rogers also found a home on television. Autry's show was an early arrival, premiering in July 1950 and staying for six years, while *The Roy Rogers Show* first aired at the tail end of 1951 and enjoyed a five-year run.

These half-hour series grew in popularity not just among young people, but with older viewers as well, encouraging the networks to venture further into western territory with "adult" oriented programs. In 1955, each of the three networks premiered an adult western: *Frontier* on NBC, *The Life and Legend of Wyatt Earp* on ABC, and *Gunsmoke* on CBS (which, like *The Lone Ranger*, began on radio). At the same time, the first hour-long western, *Cheyenne*, began its run on NBC, but only every third week, as part of the *Warner Bros. Presents* anthology. *Gunsmoke* didn't become an hour-long series until 1961.

The viewing public's enthusiasm for these westerns spurred the networks still further. By the beginning of the 1957-58 season, ABC had seven westerns on its schedule, CBS and NBC had four each. By the end of the following season, Nielsen's top four programs were, in order, *Gunsmoke, Wagon Train, Have Gun Will Travel,* and *The Rifleman.* The rest of the top 10 included *Maverick, Tales of Wells Fargo,* and *The Life and Times of Wyatt Earp.*

Still more westerns managed to squeeze their way onto the tube, reaching a saturation point during the 1959-60 season, when no fewer than *twenty-seven* westerns crammed into the three networks' prime time schedules.

It is also worth noting that television's first weekly network 90-minute drama with a regular cast was also a western. *The Virginian* premiered in September 1962 on NBC, and ran for nine years. The extended running time of each episode allowed for fuller characterizations, and played almost as a feature film each week.

But it was inevitable that the western craze would eventually burn itself out, especially with the re-emergence of the sitcom as an audience favorite. Indeed, by the 1963-64 season, there were only six westerns still left on the air among all three networks, as sitcoms placed in seven of Nielsen's top 10 series. *Bonanza* remained the only western still among the top 10.

Gunsmoke outlived all of its competitors in the genre, by remaining on the air a full 20 seasons, until its departure in 1975.

The first prime time medical drama

Medic, created by writer-producer James Moser and starring Richard Boone, premiered on September 13, 1954, on NBC. In order to create an aura of realism, the plots were based on real case histories, and the episodes were shot in real hospitals. Boone played Dr. Konrad Styner, who opened each episode with an on-camera introduction, continuing with a voice-over narration as the story unfolded. He also starred in several episodes.

The storytelling techniques employed on *Medic* gave it an unmistakable similarity to *Dragnet*'s dry, no-nonsense narrative and acting style. This was no coincidence, as James Moser also wrote the vast majority of the Dragnet scripts during the series' original 1952-57 run. Like *Dragnet*, *Medic* emphasized the procedural rather than personal aspects of its cases, but it also occasionally added a dash of creativity by presenting true-life stories from past eras. For instance, "Death Rides A Wagon," from the first season, told of how cholera was treated in the Old West. Another episode, "Dr. Impossible," dramatized medical pioneer William Stewart Halstead's search for improved surgical anesthetics in the 1880s (his experiments with cocaine injections led to his own addiction). *Medic* presented the cold, hard, and quite detailed medical facts of contemporary cases, but each episode managed to find a reasonably uplifting ending.

The program led the way for the entire medical series genre, with some shows featuring ensembles portraying hospital staffers, others focusing more narrowly on the neighborhood general practitioner. In the autumn of 1961, Moser created his second M.D. hero, *Ben Casey*. As played by Vince Edwards, Casey was, more often than not, of a rather surly demeanor, and was often satirized by comedy programs for his aloof bedside manner. But by the following spring, the show reached the Nielsen Top Ten with over 30 million viewers. It made Edwards a national sensation, and his new-found clout did not win him many friends in the business, as his reputation for being a difficult, temperamental actor grew in proportion to his popularity. There seemed to be little difference between the character and the actor who played him.

Dr. Kildare appeared on the television landscape at the same time as Ben Casey, but Kildare couldn't have been more different. Whereas Casey already had a somewhat jaded attitude when viewers were introduced to him, Kildare was still a young intern when the series premiered, and was eager to learn all he could about his profession. As Casey had a mentor in Dr. Zorba, Kildare's mentor, Dr. Gillespie, showed him the ropes of the profession. Kildare was promoted to resident in the third season.

Many more medical dramas were to come in the next few decades, including stand-out programs such as *Medical Center, Marcus Welby, M.D., Emergency, Chicago Hope,* and, of course, *ER,* the longest-running medical drama in network history (fourteen seasons).

The first prime time lawyer/legal drama

The immediate post-World War II years brought about many experimental formats among the fledgling TV stations dotted across the country, and several featured courtroom settings. In retrospect, a few of these series could be considered as the first reality shows—except that they were actually odd reality/scripted hybrids that today would defy precise labels.

In early 1946, New York's CBS station, WCBW, aired *You Be the Judge.* The show, set in a courtroom, took legal cases from the past and had three judges from the studio audience hear real lawyers represent the plaintiffs and defendants. Actors played the other roles. The studio judge who came closest to the real-life verdict won a $25.00 victory bond.

A similar format was used in *They Stand Accused,* one of the first, and perhaps most unusual series in the history of TV legal dramas. Originally produced locally in Chicago in 1949 as *Cross Question*, it was not so much a fully scripted series, but was mostly improvised by the on-camera participants as they followed the outline of a fictional case each week. The cases were created by William Wines, Assistant Attorney General for Illinois. Real-life lawyers and judges deliberated each case, with actors playing witnesses and defendants. A studio audience served as the jury, announcing its verdict at the end of the episode. It briefly aired on CBS, but moved to DuMont for the 1949-50 season, where it remained through 1954.

Yet another courtroom reality/scripted hybrid, *The Black Robe*, debuted in May of 1949. For this bizarre series, real police files and records from night court cases were used for the on-air proceedings. However, unlike later programs such as *The People's Court* and others featuring real judges and participants, *The Black Robe* did not use real-life offenders speaking for themselves. Rather, the producers roamed the streets of New York looking for average people who were asked to *portray* the real-life individuals on the show. Each of these non-actors was given a summary of the case and asked to improvise their own speaking part, as long as it stayed true to the actual arguments of the case.

Television's first *scripted* legal drama, *Mr. District Attorney*, began on radio in 1939 and first appeared on ABC for the 1951-52 season (airing on alternate Mondays with *The Amazing Mr. Malone*). It returned in syndication in 1954 for one final season. The series offered realistic treatments of stories based on true life cases, and the lead character, D.A. Paul Garrett, was supposedly a thinly fictionalized version of New York D.A. Thomas Dewey, who later became governor and presidential candidate.

The first police drama

The Plainclothesman premiered on the DuMont network on October 12, 1949, becoming the first network police drama on television. It ran for five seasons, and starred Ken Lynch—but viewers rarely saw him. Why? The show employed the subjective camera technique, in which the action is literally seen through the eyes of the protagonist—in this case, the detective referred to only as "The Lieutenant." When other characters spoke to him, the actors spoke directly into the camera. This was previously used most famously in the 1947 *film noir* theatrical feature *Lady in the Lake*, directed by and starring Robert Montgomery.

Shortly after *The Plainclothesman* first appeared (or rather, didn't appear), another DuMont network big city crime drama, *Rocky King, Inside Detective*, began its run on January 14, 1950. Roscoe Karns starred.

And, of course, there's the Methuselah of police detectives, Dick Tracy, who has tackled crime since his first appearance in the Sunday comics in 1931, and continued on radio, television, and in films. The television incarnation premiered on ABC on September 13, 1950, starring Ralph Byrd, who had also played Tracy in the film series. But the TV series had a short stay on the network, barely lasting a season before the network canceled it in February 1951. However, the program continued production in syndication under a new production company, Telescriptions, Inc., and retained the cast from ABC's version. Ralph Bird's death in August of 1952 ended production altogether. Dick Tracy reappeared, in animated form, as a kiddie cartoon produced by UPA animation studios in 1960-61.

The hearty and indisputably classic police series *Dragnet*, created by and starring Jack Webb, began on radio in 1949 and moved to TV in 1952 for a run of five years (to be resurrected in 1967 for an additional four seasons). Webb played the strait-laced Sergeant Joe Friday of the Los Angeles Police Department, narrating each episode as viewers followed him and his partner Frank Smith (Ben Alexander) as they investigated wide-ranging crimes—based on real-life cases—interviewing witnesses and suspects in clipped dialogue with nary an extraneous word between them. Another early series, *The Lineup*, followed *Dragnet's* straightforward procedural technique, but took place in San Francisco, rather than Los Angeles.

The first *female* police detective as a lead character didn't arrive on TV until September of 1974, with Sergeant "Pepper" Anderson (Angie Dickenson), who most often captured bad guys by going undercover on

NBC's *Police Woman.* Between 1981 and 1988, *Cagney and Lacey* gave TV its first female police detective team, with other women detectives following in their footsteps on series such as *Hill Street Blues,* and the various *Law & Order* incarnations.

The first private eye/detective drama

Martin Kane, Private Eye was a live half-hour series premiering on September 1, 1949, starring William Gargan. Each episode began with Kane's narration providing the necessary background information as his investigation got underway (and with the tobacco sponsor's products making their conspicuous appearance on his office desk and bookcase shelves). The *New York Times* compared the debut episode—unfavorably—to the genre of detective movie serials from which it grew. "The program suggested a grade B film that had been carefully crossed with grade C stuff, the half-hour taking in every cliché and pat situation known to the school of thrill and chill."

Despite such harsh words for the premiere installment, the series ran for five years. And, oddly enough, after the second season, Kane was played by a different actor in each of the three successive seasons—Lloyd Nolan, Lee Tracy, and finally Mark Stevens. In 1957, a new, syndicated version of the show returned, with original star Gargan back in the title role.

Private detectives were actually quite scarce on TV throughout the 1950s, but one long-running series, *Man Against Crime,* premiered on CBS just a month after *Martin Kane, Private Eye,* and ran for several seasons. The series starred Ralph Bellamy, and aired live until the beginning of the 1952 season, when it switched to film. The following year, both NBC and DuMont carried it simultaneously. It left the air for a year, and then completed its final season in 1956 as a live show once again.

Private detective series re-emerged with a vengeance—and with a new image—by the end of the 1950s. Gone was the classically cynical, hard-boiled Sam Spade type with the fedora hat, trench coat, and shabby office illuminated by an outdoor neon sign. The new crop of shows—*77 Sunset*

Anne Francis as Honey West (with pet ocelot Bruce).

Strip, Surfside 6, Hawaiian Eye, and *Checkmate* (all premiering in 1959 and 1960)—gave viewers young, attractive, well-dressed P.I.'s living quite comfortably, often in exotic locales, as the program titles indicate, and usually taking only wealthier clients.

In 1967, the more conventional old-school private detective did return, when *Mannix* began its long run on CBS. Joe Mannix worked alone and couldn't seem to go a week without taking on a case that involved a knockdown, drag-out fist fight, car chase, or both.

Over the next twenty years, private detectives on TV appeared in all shapes, sizes and genders, and employed a variety of methods to solve their cases. By the early 1970s, viewers saw overweight Frank Cannon and elderly Barnaby Jones in action, as well as blind insurance investigator Mike Longstreet, and the irrepressible Jim Rockford, who lived in a trailer by the beach, and was not immune to finding a parking ticket on his car windshield every so often.

The first series in the private-eye genre starring a female investigator, *Honey West,* appeared on TV screens in 1965. The half-hour show was based on a series of novels begun in 1957 by husband and wife team Skip and Gloria Fickling. Played with a wink and considerable smart-aleck style by Anne Francis, Honey owned a pet ocelot, was skilled in the martial arts, used sophisticated spy hardware, and often relied on her quick wit to get her out of a jam and bring down the bad guys. She was assisted by ex-Marine Sam Bolt (John Ericson).

Executive Producer Aaron Spelling, upon seeing the British hit *The Avengers,* first sought to cast that series' former co-star, Honor Blackman, as Honey. When Blackman declined the offer, Francis got the part. Alas, in a twist of fate, *Honey West* was canceled after one 30-episode season, in order for ABC to make room for their new import, *The Avengers* (co-starring Patrick Macnee and Diana Rigg, who had since replaced Blackman).

In 1976, Spelling revisited the concept of the beautiful female private eye cracking cases (and a few heads, when necessary) with far greater success, when he introduced America to *Charlie's Angels.* Despite the often cheesy plots and less-than-stellar acting, the trio of beautiful detectives (Farrah Fawcett-Majors, Kate Jackson, and Jaclyn Smith) created a national sensation, and the sky-high ratings were a major factor in boosting ABC to the top perch of the ratings for the first time in its history.

Other female private detectives on TV have since included Laura Holt in *Remington Steele*, and young but bright amateurs Nancy Drew (originally from the series of novels), and Veronica Mars.

The birth of daytime television

It behooves us to remember that regular daytime television did not begin as early in television's history as that of evening broadcasting. TV channels remained mostly blank through the daylight hours. During the war years, when it looked as if television had the potential to eventually overtake radio as a night-time entertainment medium, the unresolved question revolved around TV's ability to do the same in the daytime.

There were some holdouts on the issue of creating daytime programming. Most of the reasons for their skepticism look silly—even offensive—today. For instance, DuMont General Manager Sam Cuff predicted, "If we have daytime television, watch the divorce rate go up."

It gets worse.

Televiser magazine recounted the common arguments of the time that weighed against daytime TV, such as the assumption that the nation's women would be unable to do their housework properly and watch a television screen at the same time. Housework, presumably, would lose out. And then there were the women who would not be willing to darken their homes to the extent necessary for viewing their televisions in the daytime (before further refinement of television sets, the screens were highly susceptible to being washed out by bright sunlight). Again, it was argued, a dark house would not be conducive to housework. And thirdly, the argument went, the daytime viewing audience would be too small to attract sponsors, and would be "limited almost entirely to those who are bed-ridden, retired or institutionalized, few manufacturers would be willing to spend advertising dollars to reach such a small, unimportant audience. Without a sponsor, there would, therefore, be no network programs, and consequently, no network 'soap operas.'"

Norman D. Waters, ad agency president, and one of the founders of the American Television Society, responded to those points, beginning with his belief that daytime TV would take hold with viewers, and that televisions in the near future would not require darkened rooms for viewing. Furthermore, he argued:

> Programs on the air during the day will have to be handled
> so they can be listened to with as great interest as they can be
> watched. For example, even a woman busy with housework can
> occasionally glance at the television receiver to see what the
> artists look like, thus enabling her to get much greater enjoyment
> from the "sound" portion of the program . . . I have studied the
> habits of television set owners today, and know it to be true that
> they frequently read newspapers and books, and even play cards
> while the set is in operation. An occasional glance satisfies the
> great curiosity of the human mind concerning the appearance of
> people on television programs.

Waters concluded that lower daytime rates would attract advertisers aiming at women "who buy the lion's share of all merchandise sold to the consumer."

The daytime-or-no-daytime debate was largely put to rest on November 1, 1948, when DuMont's station WABD in New York went on the air at 7:00 a.m., with the first of several 15-minute weather and news reports for the day. Later, at 8:30, *DuMont Kindergarten* (also listed as *Baby Sitter*) debuted, with content designed to help keep pre-schoolers occupied while their mothers began the day's housework. The program, hosted by Pat Meikle, offered storytelling and drawing demonstrations, featuring a cartoon character named Wilmer the Pigeon. According to *Televisor* magazine, "Incredulous housewives and sleepy-eyed husbands could hardly believe it. But believe-it-or-not, daytime television had arrived. It was a definite milestone in television's progress . . . "

Other DuMont morning and afternoon programs appearing during that groundbreaking season included *Morning Chapel, Your Television Shopper,* and *The Needle Shop.* "Shortly after WABD went on the air with its first morning exercise," *Televiser* reported, "ABC, CBS and NBC had its own daylight programs. Of the four, DuMont's was the most extensive and perhaps most successful."

The short-lived *Telecast* magazine proclaimed, "In the years to come when historians are scribbling their chapters on television, the DuMont network will be saluted as the trail blazer...Operating without interruption from 7 a.m. until 11 p.m., this was the first TV station in the country to offer a full day's entertainment."

The first daytime soap opera on television

Many pioneering programs in the early years of TV history aired only on local stations, before the networks were established. In the case of the soap opera, or serial, the first such series to air regularly was *Vine Street*, seen on W6XAO in Los Angeles. Premiering on April 15, 1938, it was a daily, 15-minute comedy/drama starring John Barkeley and Shirley Thomas. Fifty-two episodes were aired—quite a feat, considering how few TV sets were actually in use at the time.

Several years later, other early soap operas appeared briefly as little more than blips on the TV landscape, such as the 13-part *War Bride*, which aired in the summer of 1946 on WRGB in Schenectady.

Another early but short-lived daytime soap, *These Are My Children*, originated in Chicago on January 31, 1949, airing on NBC for fifteen minutes every weekday at 5:00 p.m. The story centered on a character named Mrs. Henehan, a widow running a boarding house while raising her family. But the series was not well-received, and was cancelled less than a month after its premiere.

In late 1950, CBS attempted its first TV soap, *The First Hundred Years*, about a newlywed couple, Connie and Chris Thayer, and their next-door neighbors. The series premiered on December 4, and ended on June 27, 1952, due to low ratings. Ironically, it was replaced by another soap, *The Guiding Light*, which was brought to TV after fifteen years on radio—and continued on daytime TV for the next fifty-seven years!

Between 1950 and 1960, over forty television soaps went into production, with only six surviving the decade. Two of the survivors were the first true major network soap operas, *Search For Tomorrow* and *Love of Life*, both premiering in 1951 as daily 15-minute programs. In fact, all soaps, including those making the transition from radio (e.g. *The Guiding Light*), ran as 15-minute shows until the afternoon of April 2, 1956, when CBS debuted both *As The World Turns* and *The Edge of Night* in a 30-minute format.

The first prime time soap opera

Television's first network prime time soap opera arrived when the DuMont Network (consisting then of only New York and Washington stations) premiered *Faraway Hill*, on October 2, 1946. The serial aired on Wednesday nights at 9:00-9:30 p.m. Created by former Omaha radio producer David P. Lewis, and shot at DuMont's Wanamaker studio, the weekly story centered on wealthy New York widow Karen St. John and her unlikely romantic relationship with a country bumpkin she meets while visiting relatives. The network agreed to budget ten episodes at three hundred dollars each. After the seventh episode aired, *Television* magazine offered this assessment:

> WABC's *Faraway Hill* is one of the first attempts to put on
> a regularly scheduled television soap opera ... It has all the
> elements of let-the-soap-chips-fall-where-they-must drama with
> heartbreak, love, noble rejection, death, gossip, and plenty of
> eternal triangle ... The half-hour play moved through its scenes
> with a liberal serving of emotionalism which should satisfy the
> vast segment of the female populace with a good cry ... Good
> use was made of off-stage narration and bits of mood music to
> explain and heighten the psychological interplay of the tearful
> triangle. At the point where you felt the soap bubble was about
> to burst, a card appears proclaiming "Continued Next Week."

In the tenth episode, aired on December 18, with the network unwilling to continue the series, Lewis abruptly killed off Karen, and the series. But the potential for the soap opera was not lost on those in the industry. A postcard survey made by the Caples Company showed that out of a possible 3,600

Flora Campbell and Mel Brandt in *Faraway Hill*.

set owners, 409 had seen about three episodes of *Faraway Hill*, and the great percentage of those 409 saw an average of 5 episodes. Such figures were considered far better than comparative numbers for radio serials.

Commenting on the life and death of the program, *Televiser* magazine offered this cautiously optimistic outlook: "Will the television audience tune in a serial? Thus far there has been only one such serial telecast...and the viewer answer seems to be definitely 'yes'...The facts justify further experimentation with dramatic serials and television audience research. *Faraway Hill* has opened the door in this direction but it has only opened the door, and is interesting as a straw in the wind—not as conclusive data."

While *Faraway Hill* may have lived a brief life on television, *Hawkins Falls* (or *Hawkins Falls, Population 6,200*) was a somewhat more successful early soap. It premiered on NBC on June 17, 1950, as a prime time weekly serial drama, with stories centered on the Drewer and Corey families of Hawkins Falls, Illinois. However, the program doesn't seem to have begun as a conventional soap opera; it has been described as originally being "an odd mixture of situation comedy, light drama, and musical entertainment," with one character, newspaper editor Clate Weathers, setting up the story for each episode on camera, as his narration would lead into the dramatization.

After its initial summer run, the show was reduced to a half-hour, until it dropped off the network schedule in October. It returned in April of 1951, but as a 15-minute daytime serial, and lasted until June 1955.

Almost eighteen years after *Faraway Hill* began and ended its brief run as the first prime time network soap opera, ABC decided to take the long-established daytime serial format into the evening hours. Thus, on September 15, 1964, *Peyton Place* premiered. Based on the novel by Grace Metalious (and adapted into a 1957 feature film), the series followed the activities—romantic, criminal, and otherwise—of the residents of the fictional New England town of Peyton Place. The cast featured a slew of acting veterans and relative newcomers. The most notable young cast members who continued successful careers were Mia Farrow and Ryan O'Neal. The program aired in prime time for five seasons, and returned as a daytime serial in 1972 for two more years.

In addition to its often racy content for that era, *Peyton Place* caused a stir in the television industry by being the first major network scripted series to air twice weekly. The idea of presenting a half-hour dramatic serial on Tuesday *and* Thursday nights brought reactions of both intrigue and skepticism. Not only that, but *Peyton Place* was to air new original episodes during the summer season, while other series aired reruns. The executive producer, Paul Monash, explained that the serial nature of the show would make it impossible to interrupt the continuous storyline at any point to drop in a repeat episode.

Ratings for the program's inaugural 1964-65 season were impressive. By December, ABC had renewed it for the following season, including new summer episodes. Rumors began to spread that other twice-weekly dramas were in development, including a *Peyton Place* spinoff, *The Girl from Peyton Place*. Most of these rumors didn't amount to much, but in June 1965 the original *Peyton Place* was given a *third* timeslot each week, on Friday nights. The unprecedented move prompted NBC to make one of its most popular dramas, *Dr. Kildare*, into a twice-weekly show in its final season, airing on Monday and Tuesday each week. And a new ABC program, *Batman*,

The original cast of *Peyton Place* (l. to r.): Tim O'Connor, Mia Farrow,
Ed Nelson, Barbara Parkins, Christopher Connelly, Ryan O'Neal.

premiered in January 1966 as a Wednesday-Thursday episode tandem, with each Wednesday episode ending in a cliffhanger.

Peyton Place began to suffer a steady ratings decline in its second season, causing changes in timeslots and the eventual dropping of the third episode each week. The 1968-69 season was the program's last, and halfway through the year it was reduced to a single episode per week. Upon its cancellation, it had broadcast 514 episodes. It did find a new life, however, on the daytime schedule in 1972, where it ran for an additional two years.

In April 1978, the true Golden Age of prime time soaps was born, with the CBS premiere of future ratings titan *Dallas*. The drama, starring Larry Hagman, Victoria Principal, Linda Gray, Patrick Duffy, and countless others, centered on the wheeling-and-dealings of the wealthy Ewing family of Dallas. Hagman as the heartless, conniving J.R. Ewing became the nation's favorite TV villain. A season-ending cliffhanger in March of 1980 had an unseen assailant shoot J.R. in his office. The question "Who Shot J.R.?" consumed the nation until the November 10 episode, in which the shooter (his sister-in-law, Kristin) was revealed to a then-record 80 million viewers.

The show produced the spinoff *Knots Landing* in December of 1979. The nighttime soap genre continued to flourish with the additions of series such as short-lived *Flamingo Road, Secrets of Midland Heights*, and the far more successful *Dynasty* and *Falcon Crest*. The Fox network later found success aiming at the younger, highly-valued viewing demographic with *Beverly Hills, 90210* and *Melrose Place*. *Dawson's Creek* on the WB network also found a loyal audience among teens and twenty-somethings.

Prime time soaps in the new millennium kept the genre alive and well. ABC's *Desperate Housewives*, which, while mostly comic in nature, thrived on season-long dramatic story arcs, premiered in October 2004. *Nashville* (premiering in 2007), *The Vampire Diaries* (2009), and *Revenge* (2011), all offered continuing storylines as well.

The first miniseries

In the late 1970s, a new television form, the miniseries, took American airwaves by storm, even though it had already been a common format on British and Canadian television. The miniseries genre, also called "long form television" in the early days, distinguished itself from season-long TV series by telling a story in a pre-determined, limited number of episodes and on-air hours, rather than begin with the implied goal of running almost indefinitely. For our purposes here, we might more strictly define a miniseries as a multi-episode story consisting of at least three episodes or hours, airing on consecutive nights, or in a weekly time slot, until its conclusion.

The Forsyte Saga first aired on the BBC in 1967, and made its debut on NET (before it transformed into PBS) during the 1969-70 season. Another high profile British miniseries, *Elizabeth R,* aired in the U.S. in 1973. That same year, an American production, *The Blue Knight,* adapted from the Joseph Wambaugh novel, aired as a four-hour presentation.

QBVII, based on the 1970 novel by Leon Uris and produced by Screen Gems, featured an all-star cast including Ben Gazzara and Anthony Hopkins. The story of a real-life British libel court case premiered on ABC beginning April 29, 1974. It aired all of its six hours on two consecutive nights, prompting many TV historians to deem it first American miniseries. But, like *The Blue Knight,* it could also be considered more accurately as a somewhat lengthy two-part presentation, rather than a true "series" airing in a regular time slot on successive nights, or weeks.

However, the miniseries that truly launched a tremendous, industry-wide trend in television in the late 1970s was *Rich Man, Poor Man* on ABC. The sprawling, 12-hour series followed the wildly divergent lives of the Jordache brothers— wealthy, aspiring politician Rudy, and down-on-his luck boxer Tom—from their late teens well into adulthood. Peter Strauss, Nick Nolte, Edward Asner, and Susan Blakely starred. The miniseries premiered on February 1, 1976, with a two-hour installment, followed by hour-long episodes airing each week until late March. It was a ratings smash, with every episode landing in the Nielsen ratings Top Ten, averaging more than 40% of the viewing audience.

Rich Man, Poor Man (left to right: Peter Strauss as Rudy Jordache, Susan Blakely as his wife Julie, and Nick Nolte as Tom Jordache.

ABC had been developing both *QBVII* and *Rich Man, Poor Man* for several years before their premieres. *TV Guide* reported back in July of 1972 that the network had just acquired the rights to both novels (the magazine also had the foresight at the time to refer to the budding projects as "miniseries)."

The day after the concluding episode of *Rich Man, Poor Man* aired, TV writer Les Brown wrote in *The New York Times* that the presentation "has left television permanently changed . . . Ironically, the program was such a runaway hit that it will unquestionably be turned into a regular series next fall, whereupon it will have to revert to format." Indeed, the story continued the following season as a more conventional weekly series, *Rich Man, Poor Man, Book II.*

Perhaps even more significantly, 1977 saw the landmark airing of *Roots.* ABC took an even bigger gamble by scheduling this miniseries, dramatizing author Alex Haley's family history from slavery through the end of the Civil War, to air on eight *consecutive* nights, beginning on January 23. The gamble paid off in historic proportions. It was estimated that 100 million viewers saw all or part of *Roots*, making it the most-watched television drama of any kind ever broadcast.

With that sort of off-the-chart success, the miniseries format quickly became prominent on the networks, with each new presentation highly touted more as an event than as a mere TV program. CBS director of its miniseries division, Michael Sevareid, reported in September of 1977 that "I've seen scripts for Jewish *Roots*, Italian *Roots*, and Indian *Roots*...we're trying to stay away from generation-type novels." Instead, CBS aired *The Dain Curse*, a 6-hour adaptation of the Dashiell Hammett novel.

Over at NBC, miniseries presentations included an adaptation of James Michener's *Centennial*, the soapy *79 Park Avenue*, and the weighty *Holocaust*, with an all-star cast, featuring an up-and-coming New York stage actress named Meryl Streep.

ABC's other big miniseries included *How the West Was Won*, starring longtime *Gunsmoke* hero James Arness. *The Winds of War* and its sequel, *War and Remembrance*, both starring Robert Mitchum, also received considerable hype and high ratings. In addition, the political intrigue of *Washington Behind Closed Doors*, based on former Watergate conspirator John Ehrlichman's novel *The Company*, exceeded even *Roots* in ambitious scheduling, by airing all twelve hours over six consecutive nights.

But the combination of expense and the rise of cable networks contributed to the fall of the broadcast network miniseries, and later examples usually took the form of two-part movies, thus reverting back to the original format of *QBVII*, and, in a way, bringing the miniseries full-circle.

The first rotating series on TV

In the late 1960s, an interesting variation of the weekly network drama series first appeared. Some clusters of new programs joined the prime time schedule under an umbrella title, but were sub-divided into three or four individual series, rotating with each other every few weeks.

In September of 1968, *The Name of the Game* (based on the 1966

TV-movie *Fame is the Name of the Game*) began its regular run on NBC, with three rotating lead characters: Glenn Howard (Gene Barry), owner of a worldwide publishing empire, and two of his most valued employees—Jeff Dillon (Tony Franciosa), a young, hot-shot investigative reporter for Howard's *People* magazine (before there was the real-life *People* magazine) and Dan Farrell (Robert Stack), a former FBI agent-turned-editor of *Crime* magazine. Each lead actor would take his turn receiving top billing for an episode with his own plotline, while the others would briefly appear in cameos, if at all. The one character common to all three was secretary Peggy Maxwell (Susan St. James). The series was also notable for being among the handful of weekly 90-minute dramas in television history.

A year after *The Name of the Game* premiered, *The Bold Ones* arrived, with three of its own separate, self-contained rotating series: *The New Doctors, The Lawyers,* and *The Protectors* (later replaced by *The Senator*). By 1973, only *The New Doctors* was left standing before its own cancellation.

The most successful rotating series, *NBC Mystery Movie,* began its run in September 1971, with *Columbo, McMillian & Wife,* and *McCloud* taking turns in the time slot. Their popularity prompted NBC to add another night of rotating mystery series, moving the original to Sunday and re-naming it *The NBC Sunday Mystery Movie.* The new set of series, airing on Wednesdays, consisted of *Madigan, Cool Million,* and *Banacek.* Of these, only *Banacek* won the approval of viewers, and was given its own weekly, 90-minute time slot in September 1972. A year after *Quincy* joined the Sunday rotation, it became a stand-alone, one-hour series in September 1977.

An earlier television experiment of a slightly different kind, involving three separate series under one umbrella title, appeared briefly on NBC in 1964-65. The title *90 Bristol Court* filled a 90-minute time slot on Monday nights, but was comprised of three separate sitcoms airing consecutively: *Karen* (starring Debbie Watson as a trouble-prone 16-year-old), *Harris Against the World* (Jack Klugman as a harried family man), and *Tom, Dick and Mary* (Tom Galloway, Joyce Bulifant, and Steve Franken as young hospital employees who also live together). The one and only thing the three series had in common was their setting—an apartment complex tended by handyman Cliff Murdoch, the only character to appear in each of the three series. But both *Harris Against the World* and *Tom, Dick and Mary* were cancelled by January, leaving *Karen* to survive on its own for the rest of the season. Had the creators chosen to have the characters of each series interact with each other to some degree (as neighbors are known to do) it might have made the 90-minute block more interesting. But most critics at the time couldn't find much to say in a positive vein about the individual programs.

The first TV reality program

Reality programs have come in many forms and have created a multitude of sub-genres since the early 1990s, so a reasonably specific definition of "reality program" would be in order here. We can define a reality program (not including documentary or man-on-the-street formats) as a TV entertainment program in which most or all of the performers are *not* playing fictional characters, but rather themselves, and are not reciting from a written script (although in recent years it has become common for producers to "create" seemingly spontaneous situations in which the participants would react).

One of the strongest contenders for the title of First Reality Program is the old reliable practical joke program *Candid Camera,* which first aired on ABC as *Candid Microphone* in August of 1948. It became *Candid Camera* upon switching networks to NBC the following year. The premise of the show—using hidden cameras to watch unsuspecting people encounter and react to unexpected and/or bizarre situations—was a simple but endlessly entertaining early example of observing real people being themselves under unlikely circumstances. The program—created, produced, and hosted by Alan Funt—enjoyed a run of over forty years on and off, and in various incarnations, both in daytime and evening time slots. Upon Funt's death, his son Peter assumed hosting chores, and, in 2014, returned with yet another new *Candid Camera* incarnation, with actress Mayim Bialik as co-host.

However, most of us have come to think of reality shows as those following a person or group of "real" people—either celebrities, semi-celebrities, or total unknowns—on a weekly basis, as they make their way through their lives, well aware that their words and actions are being recorded.

In January of 1973, PBS presented the first of this style of reality series, *An American Family*, a real-life program with what was then considered a somewhat baffling concept for a TV series. For this 12-part weekly program, hand-held cameras followed the daily activities of the well-to-do Loud family of Santa Barbara, California, as they lived their daily lives. The program was conceived and produced by Craig Gilbert, who provided an on-camera introduction opening the first episode: "The Louds are neither average nor typical. No family is. They are not *the* American family, they are simply *an* American family." Filming took place between May 30 and December 31, 1971. Over 300 hours of raw footage were shot by filmmakers Alan and Susan Raymond. There was no host, no interviews, and very little voice-over narration.

What was *not* anticipated during the show's production was the actual dissolution of William and Pat Loud's marriage, which was filmed for the entire nation to see. The premiere episode opened with the final day of filming, as the family prepared for a New Year's Eve party—the parents had been separated for four months by then.

In addition, one of their sons, Lance, announced he was gay during the filming—something definitely uncommon on prime time television in 1973. "... By openly airing their personal crises on camera," reflected *TV Guide*, "[the Louds] turned themselves into performers and turned viewers into voyeurs."

Critic Cleveland Amory wrote: "In a word, the producer was lucky. With the separation, which he didn't know would happen, the show works. Without it, the idea of spending an hour a week for 12 weeks with Mr. and Mrs. William C. Loud of Santa Barbara, California, their five children, their ranch house, their swimming pool and their four foreign cars would have all the appeal of watching 12 hours of—well, Mr. and Mrs. William C. Loud's home movies."

The series was parodied by Albert Brooks in his 1979 feature film comedy *Real Life*, starring Charles Grodin, with Brooks playing a director desperate to film something of interest in the everyday life of Grodin's onscreen family.

The early 1980s saw the first true surge of programs featuring "average" people rather than professional actors. These programs, such as *Real People, That's Incredible,* and even *Those Amazing Animals,* were all studio based and taped with a live audience, and were hosted by affable, chatty TV personalities of somewhat dubious celebrity credentials. The shows presented reality programming in the form of brief human interest stories, ranging from uplifting to just plain strange—and usually comical. "Viewers seemed to respond to almost any show that focused its cameras on what was taking place outside the studios and sound stages of Hollywood," *Panorama* magazine reported. And, as *Real People* producer George Schlatter explained at the time, "I think we were getting a little bored with the same situation comedies, the same specials, the same performers you see on all the talk shows. *Real People* gives you a chance to see some different people, people you can relate to. And it makes you feel good: it show you heroes, role models. I don't think you have that anyplace else on television."

Some critics had the same problem with the first generation of reality shows back then as they would twenty years later. "The problem seems to be," wrote Cyra McFadden in 1980, "that in front of TV cameras, real people cease to be real. Self-consciousness sets in, or the ham in us, or unconscious imitation of the slickees we see on the screen—personalities rather than people."

But it wouldn't be until the late 1980s and early 1990s when the real avalanche of reality programs would nearly consume network TV programming. One trend-setting example, *Cops,* premiered on the Fox network in 1989, with its *cinéma verité* style providing many adrenaline-pumping (and a few unintentionally comical) moments as camera crews followed real police from the Dade County, Florida, sheriff's department on their patrol assignments, answering calls ranging from domestic squabbles to pursuing suspects on foot and in high-speed car chases. With that series' success, and its expansion to include the lives of patrol police in other cities, more reality programs began to appear. Some of these consisted of little more than having cameras roll during private moments among the participants, whether anything of significance was happening or not. An early example, *The Real World,* directly inspired by *An American Family,* premiered in 1992.

The year 2000 brought another wave of reality shows such as *Big Brother* and *Survivor*, the latter created with a framework of an extended competition among two "tribes" of competitors isolated in various remote tropical locales for six weeks at a time. Physical endurance contests and races, sometimes with fresh food as the prize, gave the participants more to do when they weren't baring their souls, their bodies (most being quite young and fit), strategizing, or lapsing into mundane conversation on camera.

The singing competition *American Idol* also debuted in 2000. *The Amazing Race*—with ten to twelve teams of two literally racing each other around the world—premiered the following year. Due to the low cost of producing programs that didn't require scriptwriters, high-profile actors, multiple sets, and all that goes into producing conventional dramas or sitcoms, the reality genre exploded across the television landscape. All manner of celebrities—be they actors or singers somewhat past their career peak, or "famous" people with little if any justification for their dubious fame—seemed to be considered choice subjects for having their everyday lives recorded for posterity by a camera crew.

The abundance of reality programs prompted the addition of the Emmy Award category "Outstanding Reality Program" in 2001, which was tweaked in 2003 and renamed "Outstanding Reality-Competition Program," in order to include both the fly-on-the-wall and competition-style programs (*The Amazing Race* won this category for its first seven consecutive years). In 2008, the academy added the category "Outstanding Host for a Reality or Reality-Competition Program."

The next decade saw the arrivals and departures of countless reality and reality-competition programs, some of which would have difficulty justifying their very existence on television. The field became so crowded as to prompt the Television Academy to fine tune its categories yet again. By 2015, the "Outstanding Reality-Competition Program" title (covering programs such as *The Amazing Race, Dancing with the Stars, Project Runway, So You Think You Can Dance, The Voice*), had been further divided into "Outstanding Structured Reality Program" (e.g. *Antiques Roadshow, Mythbusters, Shark Tank, Undercover Boss*), and "Outstanding Unstructured Reality Program" (*Alaska, The Last Frontier, Intervention, Deadliest Catch*).

The first children's TV show

Before *Kukla, Fran, and Ollie* and *Howdy Doody* became synonymous with early children's television, and later as favorite sources of nostalgia and trivia questions for the original generation of baby-boomers, there was the DuMont Network's *Small Fry Club*, which began as a local radio program in Massachusetts in 1921 (early even in radio's history). It debuted as a TV program on March 11, 1947 (to be fair, *Howdy Doody* also premiered in 1947, but not until December 27).

A few children's programs had appeared even earlier in local markets, such as *Children's Matinee*, which first aired in March 1940 on New York's W2XBS. In 1942, WRGB in Schenectady experimented with *Children's Story*, *Stories for the Nursery*, and *The Children's Hour*. But *Small Fry Club* was the first network program for kids, and host Bob Emery was the first of the "big brother" children's show hosts—affable, comforting, often singing and playing his ukulele on the show. Entertainment historian Andrew Fielding notes that Emery played ukulele as did Cliff Edwards (better known as "Ukulele Ike") and Arthur Godfrey—probably, writes Fielding, because "the instrument suggests an intimacy of performance. There was much room in early TV for performers who sought to establish—either with an instrument such as the ukulele, or without—a personal, intimate sense."

Emery often used the teaching tool of having the program's on-air kids make drawings illustrating the best ways of behaving, and he spoke about such simple life lessons as eating a balanced breakfast and brushing teeth. He also introduced cartoon segments, created by Van Bueren Studios. A case could be made that Emery's agreeable demeanor and rapport with children served as a template for many classic children's programs to follow, including *Romper Room*, Paul Tripp's *Mr. I. Magination*, *Sesame Street*, and especially Fred Rogers's much-loved *Mr. Rogers' Neighborhood*.

Small Fry Club was the first to encourage viewer mail, hold write-in contests, and offer membership to its fan club, partly to gauge the size and loyalty of the viewing audience. Emery attracted over 150,000 club members by 1950, indicating that over 75% of the TV viewing audience at the time watched *Small Fry Club*.

The show ran five days a week—one of the first entertainment programs to do so—and was televised from DuMont's main studio on Madison Avenue (which, due to the limited budget, was basically one large room divided into individual sets for its different programs). *Small Fry Club* ran for four years, ending on June 15, 1951.

Another very early program for young people, *Rumpus Room* (originally on radio as *Johnny Olsen's Rumpus Room*) first aired on DuMont's WABD in New York in late 1946. Judging by descriptions of the time, the program had a variety format aimed more at teens than younger children, with a good deal of airtime devoted to music and dancing, courtesy of a large jukebox placed prominently on the set (think of it as a sort of hybrid between future favorites *Wonderama* and *American Bandstand*). Johnny Olsen, who would later gain fame mostly off-camera as a ubiquitous game show announcer, presided over the activities on *Rumpus Room*, which included interviews with the kids, comedy gags, phone-in quizzes for prize money, and celebrity guests.

The first animated cartoon ever shown on TV

Walt Disney's 7-minute Donald Duck short, *Donald's Cousin Gus* appeared on screens in New York as part of NBC's first night of television programming, on May 3, 1939, just a few days after television's "official" first day at the World's Fair. Not only was *Donald's Cousin Gus* the first cartoon to air, but by virtue of being on film, it became one of the first pre-recorded program to appear on TV.

The first made-for-TV cartoon

The first cartoon produced especially for television was *Crusader Rabbit*, which premiered on the NBC Los Angeles affiliate on September 1, 1949.

The show was the creation of animator Alex Anderson and producer Jay Ward (later of *Rocky and Bullwinkle* fame). They first joined forces in 1947 to create Television Arts Productions, and pitched *Crusader Rabbit* to NBC as part of the series *The Comic Strips of Television*. After the pilot episode aired in Los Angeles, the program was not chosen for network distribution, but was instead syndicated to individual stations (although some of those stations were NBC affiliates).

Crusader Rabbit's animation was barely animation at all, but rather consisted mostly of still drawings with only occasional motion, due to the low budget the series had to work with. A narrator guided the story along and occasionally spoke to directly to Crusader Rabbit, who jumped into action when necessary.

The series produced 195 black-and-white episodes and 260 color episodes, many of which were written in serial form, including cliffhangers to keep viewers tuning in.

The first *fully* animated program produced especially for television was *Huckleberry Hound*, created by animation veterans William Hannah and Joseph Barbera and voiced by Daws Butler. It debuted on October 2, 1958, and became the first animated program to win an Emmy award. It also led to the first cartoon spinoff on TV, *The Yogi Bear Show*, in 1961.

Cartoons that were originally produced as theatrical shorts for movie theaters also became extremely popular on TV in the 1950s. In September of 1956, 234 Popeye cartoons, along with several Warner Brothers shorts, were sold to Associated Artist Productions to be syndicated, for a reported $2.4 million. That same year, CBS bought the rights to all of Terrytoon cartoons, which included the popular *Heckle & Jeckle* series. They were packaged in a prime time, 13-week summer program, *CBS Cartoon Theatre*, hosted by a relative unknown actor/comedian named Dick van Dyke.

The ever-popular Warner Brothers cartoons from the post-World War II years, featuring Bugs Bunny, Daffy Duck, Porky Pig and others (all voices performed by Mel Blanc) didn't arrive on TV until October of 1960, with the prime time *Bugs Bunny Show*, airing on Tuesdays at 7:30 p.m., with newly-created links between the individual cartoons. The final first-run episode aired in August of 1962. It then moved to Saturday mornings and remained there in various incarnations (including joining forces with *The Road Runner Show*) for the next forty years.

The first animated sitcom

Decades before *The Simpsons* premiered as a half-hour sitcom on the Fox network (having first appeared as short cartoons on *The Tracy Ullman Show*), *The Flintstones* became the first prime-time animated sitcom, premiering on September 30, 1960, on ABC, in the Friday 8:30-9:00 p.m. timeslot, and ran for six full seasons. The characters Fred and Wilma Flintstone (voiced by Alan Reed and Jean VanderPyl), and their neighbors Barney and Betty Rubble (Mel Blanc and Bea Benaderet) were loosely based on Jackie Gleason's tremendously popular sitcom *The Honeymooners.* In its final season, 1966, *The Flintsones* won a Golden Globe Award for "Outstanding Achievement in International Television."

Another Hanna and Barbera creation, *The Jetsons*, premiered in ABC's prime time in September of 1962, on Sunday evenings. Whereas *The Flintstones* took place in the Stone Age, *The Jetsons* was set on the opposite end of the timeline, in the distant, space-age future. The Jetsons family was headed by George (George O'Hanlon) and Jane (voiced by Penny Singleton, best known for her starring role in the 1940s *Blondie* film series).

It may come as a surprise that *The Jetsons* lasted only a single season in its original run—due mostly to its competition, *Disney's Wonderful World of Color* on NBC—although it did live on in syndication on Saturday mornings, for which a new batch of episodes was produced in 1985.

In September 1972, the half-hour animated sitcom, *Wait Till Your Father Gets Home*, was syndicated and often aired in prime time, riding the coattails of the new permissiveness on TV spawned by *All in the Family.*

When *The Simpsons* became a half-hour prime time sitcom in 1989, it was the sole occupant of that genre for over seven years, until a new crop of animated comedies appeared. Mike Judge, creator of MTV's notorious *Beavis and Butthead*, followed that cult favorite with *King of the Hill* in 1997. Later that same year, the controversial, envelope-pushing *South Park* premiered on Comedy Central. And, in 1999, two more animated sitcoms, *Family Guy* and *Futurama* joined the Fox Network's prime time schedule.

However, *The Simpsons* has since earned the title of "Longest Running

American Sitcom of All-Time." It will have aired over 600 episodes by the end of the 2015-16 season.

The first TV series adapted from a comic strip

In 1949, *Li'l Abner*, created by Al Capp in 1934, came close to becoming the first comic strip adapted as a television series, but didn't quite make it. Craig Shepard and Judy Bourne were cast as Abner and Daisy Mae, after winning their roles as part of a nationwide talent search. The process got as far as having publicity photos taken of the stars in character, but the series never aired.

So, the honor goes to *Buck Rogers*. The title character first appeared in a story by Philip Francis Nowland titled "Armageddon, 2419 A.D.," printed in the August 1928 issue of *Amazing Stories*. *Buck Rogers* became a regular comic strip the following year, and, in 1939, was adapted into a 12-part film serial starring Buster Crabbe. Buck arrived on TV as a half-hour weekly ABC series in April 1950, but the show lasted only until January of 1951 (twenty-eight years later, it was revived in 1979 by NBC for a two-year run).

Two years after Buck Rogers's arrival on TV, Superman found a home on the small screen in *The Adventures of Superman*, beginning a syndicated run in 1952. The character, created by Jerry Siegel and Joe Shuster, first appeared in *Action Comics #1* in 1938. In 1941, movie audiences saw an animated Superman fighting on behalf of the war effort, and in 1948, he appeared in the first of two live-action serials starring Kirk Alyn, with Noel Neill as Lois Lane. The TV series, *The Adventures of Superman*, starred George Reeves, Neill, Jack Larson, and John Hamilton.

Not every comic strip character to get his or her own TV series has been a superhero, like Flash Gordon, Wonder Woman, or the Incredible Hulk. Adaptations of more genteel comic strips, such as *Dennis the Menace* and *Hazel*, also found considerable success on the tube. *Dennis the Menace*, created by Hank Ketchum, first appeared in newspapers in March of 1951, and became a series in 1959, starring Jay North as Dennis. A television version of the *Blondie* comic strip reached television in January of 1957, with Arthur Lake reprising his film series role as Dagwood Bumstead, with Pamela

Britton as Blondie. The series lasted a single season. *Hazel*, created by Ted Key, first appeared in the *Saturday Evening Post* in 1943, and joined the TV line-up in 1961 for a five-year run, with Oscar-winner Shirley Booth starring as Hazel. And the ghoulish Addams Family, created by Charles Addams as a single-panel comic, came to life on television in 1964.

Conversely, there have also been TV series that spawned their own comic strips. For instance, the dashing young Dr. Kildare had a life extending beyond the confines of the TV screen. His first film appearance came in *Interns Can't Take Money* (1937), with Joel McCrea as Kildare, and Lionel Barrymore as his mentor, Dr. Gillespie. Lew Ayres took over for McCrea for the next nine films in the series. After 1942, the series shifted its focus to Gillespie. The TV series, starring Richard Chamberlain, premiered in 1961, soon to be accompanied by a comic strip version by Ken Bald, which began its long run the following year. How long? The TV series ended its five-year run in 1966, but the comic strip continued until 1983!

Even the prime time soap *Dallas* found its way onto the comics pages in 1981, when New Jersey cartoonist and *Dallas* fan Jim Lawrence collaborated with Los Angeles artist Ron Harris to create new stories for the Ewing clan. The strip was distributed by *The Los Angeles Times* Syndicate to about 350 newspapers. But due to the serial nature of the TV show and its multiple storylines, the comic strip had to be carefully written and presented, so as not to contradict or duplicate the storylines of the series. Lawrence and Harris had to constantly check with *Dallas* production company, Lorimar, and submit storylines in advance. "The strip only ran one story at a time," Lawrence explained. "A comic strip is a terribly circumscribed art form. We're crystal simplicity itself compared with the content of the show."

The first TV game/quiz show

Game and quiz programs, immensely popular on radio since the mid-1930s, have been a part of TV programming since the pre-World War II years. While several popular radio game shows were among the first programs to make the transition to television, other early examples were created specifically for the tube.

The first game/quiz show to appear on any TV station was *Spelling Bee*, which aired locally on WRGB in Schenectady in 1940. Slides showed the correct spelling of each word to the viewing audience.

On July 1, 1941, the very first day of FCC-approved commercial television, two stations in New York signed on the air, WNBT (NBC) and WCBW (CBS). On that day, WNBT broadcast TV versions of two popular radio game shows, *Uncle Jim's Question Bee*, hosted by Jim McWilliams, and *Truth or Consequences*, hosted by Ralph Edwards. But it was a one-time broadcast for each, solely to commemorate the first day of commercial TV broadcasting. *Truth or Consequences* wouldn't begin its regular television run for another nine years. On the following day, July 2, the hour-long *CBS Television Quiz* began airing live each week from the CBS studios at Grand Central Station, and stayed on the air for over a year.

Ladies Be Seated, a stunt show created by Ralph Edwards, first came to TV from radio on February 24, 1945. The host was Johnny Olsen, later known also as the announcer for several other game shows, such as *The Price Is Right*. Harvey Marlowe, Executive Television Director at ABC, explained that in order to enhance the show's chances of success for *Ladies Be Seated* on television, "only strong visual gags were used, resulting in one of the best-rated video shows to date. Johnny Olsen and *Ladies Be Seated* was presented for a 13-week series over WRGB, Schenectady, and on various occasions at WABD, New York, WPTZ, Philadelphia, and WBKB, Chicago. In other words, the show has played the ABC circuit."

Play the Game, a charades show featuring semi-celebrities as participants, described at the time as having an informal, house party atmosphere, began in New York in 1946, and was produced by ABC, but was seen on DuMont. In 1948, when ABC began full-time network broadcasting, *Play the Game* switched over to that network, lasting only another few months.

It should be noted that most of these post-war game shows, along with others such as *Cash and Carry*, and *See What You Know*, cannot be considered true successes; each lasted a very brief time on the air. But they helped the game show genre get its sea legs on TV. And, they gained strength in numbers and in popularity throughout the next decade—until the infamous Quiz Show Scandal of 1958.

The first TV talk show host

The first TV station in Los Angeles, KTLA, was founded by Don Lee in 1931 as W6XYZ. Shortly thereafter, a young writer named Franklin Lacey began a simple talk show on which he'd have one-on-one conversations with celebrity guests. The show had very few viewers—perhaps only a few dozen—but Lacey got top-name entertainers to join him for his hour-long chats, and he even occasionally accepted invitations to bring his guests to a viewer's home after the show.

Several of network television's earliest talk show hosts were women. Martha Rountree, a journalist and radio producer who created *Meet the Press* for radio in 1945, served as moderator for the program from its inception through its move to the NBC television network in 1947 (at the time, the network consisted of the New York and Washington, D.C. affiliates). She remained with the show until 1953, and has been the only female host in the program's long history.

In the fall of 1948, two other talk shows premiered, each with a female host, and each designed for a largely female viewership. The CBS daytime interview program *Vanity Fair* debuted in October, hosted by news reporter Dorothy Doan. It aired twice a week for its first month, then every weekday beginning in November. It moved among a number of daytime time slots until its cancellation in 1951.

Radio favorite Mary Margaret McBride, who thrived on daytime radio throughout the 1940s with her casual, mid-western manner and sensibilities, also ventured onto television in the fall of 1948, with a half-hour prime time interview show. She did not fare well, however, and lasted less than two months. Speculation at the time attributed this to the increased male audience in the evening, which wasn't as enamored of McBride as was her daytime radio audience of housewives.

But male viewers could be credited in no small part for the success of another woman, Faye Emerson, who, in 1950, became one of network television's

Faye Emerson.

talk show pioneers. An actress known for her glamorous taste in fashion, including her notoriously plunging necklines, Emerson was also noteworthy for her five-year marriage to Franklin Roosevelt's son, Elliot. Her close Hollywood and Washington connections enabled her to invite a variety of high-profile celebrity guests on her 15-minute talk show. The program aired in various time slots and networks throughout 1950, during which she invited guests to chat about show business and/or gossip that had been making the rounds in the entertainment field. Emerson hosted other local and network shows in the early 1950s as well, and was frequently seen as a game show panelist.

The first musical/variety special

On September 28, 1944, *Esquire* magazine sponsored an elaborate musical production, *The Boys From Boise*, on WABD in New York, to the tune of $10,000, and hyped in print ads as "the first full-length television musical comedy written and produced expressly for television." And so it was. The story of a chorus troupe stranded on a ranch used 44 performers and 11 musicians, and ran over two hours in length—all live, of course.

Raymond Nelson, vice-president of the Charles M. Storm Co., the advertising agency supervising the production, chose a baking metaphor to explain how the undertaking gained momentum. "We didn't have any recipe, or precedent, to go by, but we were sure of our ingredients and our ability to mix them, and we had baked in a television studio—literally and figuratively—a hundred times."

The ambitious production of *The Boys from Boise*."

Due to the sheer size and ambition of the production, the cast, musicians, and sets had to be carefully maneuvered throughout the cramped studio, making sure no single bit of studio space was wasted.

"We figured out the studio dimensions to the last square foot," Nelson explained, "because the orchestra occupied part of the space into which cameras would ordinarily back for long shots. And there was the problem of getting directions from the control room to cameramen who were working in the midst of an almost constant blast of sound."

Actually, two studios were used—the second floor main studio for the production itself, and the 42nd floor studio for the live commercials.

Rehearsals for the show were not without a few minor setbacks: due to the intensity of the studio lights, one of the female extras passed out from heat prostration and had to be carried off the set. Another extra accidentally knocked over a mike boom. But the live broadcast went off without a hitch.

Despite the reasonably impressive outcome of such a complex production, *The Boys from Boise* didn't exactly light up the young TV industry. *Television* magazine mused at the time that "the length could have been cut advantageously to a half hour with a much smaller cast. But the publicity value was the thing, so it served its purpose in that respect."

The *New York Times* review gave the production credit for taking a big step in television's development, for the financial investment involved, and for dealing with wartime limitations. But the imperfections couldn't be ignored.

> If nothing else, the show was too ambitious and too long for
> its own good, because inevitably a "musical comedy" will
> seem pretty static when the cameras and receiving screen will
> encompass only four girls at a time and then without enough
> room to permit real dancing . . . . It was more in the solo numbers
> that *The Boys from Boise* came into its own and showed what
> television will be able to do. Gwen Davis had a torchy ballad,
> "Broken Hearted Blues" to render and she did it superbly . . . For
> a few minutes then, there was the warmth and action associated
> with the theatre and films, and so sadly lacking in radio . . .

The production was also acknowledged as a formidable example of television's demands from its performers, i.e. actors who can memorize lines and offer a quality performance throughout the length of the show. Finally, there was praise for the placement of advertisements between the acts, preventing unnecessary interruptions to the flow of the story.

For all of its imperfections, the production did provide useful experience for those responsible for planning, rehearsing, and executing future live spectaculars for the small screen.

The first weekly prime time variety program

Hour Glass was the first weekly—and first hour-long—variety series on television, premiering on May 9, 1946, on NBC. At a time when there were still precious few TV sets in private homes across the country (with more than half of those in the New York City area), and with programs broadcast sporadically and on shoestring budgets, *Hour Glass* provided the first real glimpse of television's potential as an entertainment medium. The sponsor, Standard Brands—makers of Chase & Sanborn Coffee and Tender-leaf Tea—provided an extravagant budget for the show, resulting in elaborate sets and top-name entertainers. And, because at that time, a sponsor's advertising agency controlled the production and content of each time slot it had purchased, the J. Walter Thompson agency assigned a staff to write and produce Hour Glass each week. The agency paid all production staff salaries, and worked with a budget of about $3,000 for each week's program, about half of which would go towards scenery, costumes, and props. Segments each week included one-act dramatic plays, comedy sketches, singing performances, and short films.

Television magazine assessed the sponsor's lavish budget for the show thusly: . . .

> When the announcement was made that Standard Brands had signed for a series of television variety shows, there was a lot of speculation about why a company so wise in the expenditure of advertising dollars had contracted for an expensive series over WNBT in the face of the admittedly limited circulation. What

were the reasons behind this move . . . and what return was expected? The answer is not too difficult to find if one glances back sixteen odd years ago and finds that Standard Brands was one of the earliest to appreciate the value. Ever hear of Charlie McCarthy, *One Man's Family*, or Fred Allen? The corporation well realize the proven advantage of finding the right time and the right outlet for the right show. *Hour Glass* over WNBT produced by J. Walter Thompson, is their attempt to find the television answer . . .

The host throughout most of the program's 10-month run was Helen Parrish, who received a good deal of press for her engaging personality, and who inspired the short-lived term "femcee."

"It is felt that by building her up," noted *Television* magazine, "the Standard Brands show will also benefit. Miss Parrish has been an actress on the stage and on radio prior to her choice for this important role of femceeing this hour-long show." Parrish received $250 a week for her femceeing.

In its first few months on the air, the program's individual segments had no unifying theme, but by the fall, the goal leaned towards weaving each hour's content together by story or locale, which also helped incorporating the commercial interludes more smoothly. Producers Ed Rice and Harry Hermann worked independently, each producing a show every other week, with his own set of writers.

Guest stars along the way included Bert Lahr, Peggy Lee, and Edgar Bergen, who was among the first radio comedians to dip his toe into television's waters. Bergen appeared on *Hour Glass* on November 14, 1946, along with his wooden friends Charlie McCarthy, Mortimer Snerd and Effie Klinker. But at least one reviewer remained underwhelmed. "It proved once more," *Time* magazine grumbled, "that television has a long way to go even to catch up with radio's form of entertainment...The only time this crew struck a familiar spark of humor was when Bergen dusted off a vaudeville routine, playing doctor to McCarthy's unrealized tonsillectomy. Otherwise, he floundered vaguely in the unfamiliarity of a television set."

The first late-night variety program

Once the networks had fully beefed up their prime time schedules by 1950, the content of the later hours, especially from 10:00 p.m. onward, were dubbed "late-night" programs.

The first of these was NBC's *Broadway Open House*, an energetic, fast-moving variety show originally hosted alternately by comedians Jerry Lester and Morey Amsterdam. It aired every weeknight, premiering on May 29, 1950, in the 10:00-11:00 p.m. time slot. Amsterdam hosted on Mondays and Wednesdays, and Lester on Tuesdays, Thursdays, and Fridays. Amsterdam left the show in the early goings, leaving Lester as sole host. An average program consisted of comedy sketches, guest singers, and audience participation bits.

A year after the show's premiere, a new character was added to the stable of performers—a young, well-endowed blonde named Dagmar (stage name: Jennie Lewis, born Virginia Ruth Egnor), who, playing a stereotypical dumb blonde, took television by storm. Her popularity was such that Lester reportedly began to resent the media paying so much attention to her (including a *Life* magazine cover story), and ultimately left the show because of it. The program ended altogether a month later.

Broadway Open House inspired a new television genre, the late-night talk/variety show, which eventually found its niche in the post-11:00 p.m. hours, after local newscasts. Former NBC president Sylvester "Pat" Weaver, who created *The Today Show* in 1952, also created its opposite, late-night bookend *The Tonight Show* in 1954, with Steve Allen as host. As Weaver explained years later, "We had a late-night show on called *Broadway Open House*, with Jerry Lester and Morey Amsterdam, that was a runaway hit. I knew from radio that there was a big late-night audience. I wanted *The Tonight Show* to be a comedy-cum-coverage show that would entertain but also cover the whole field of entertainment: what's opening, what's closing, who's playing at the Martinique ... We did *The Tonight Show* live from the Hudson Theatre in Times Square. Steve Allen had an orchestra and special guests and his own people, like Don Knotts ... "

Allen left *The Tonight Show* in 1957 in favor of a prime time slot, and thereafter, beginning with the Jack Paar years (1957-62), the program faced

Typical shenanigans on *Broadway Open House*:
Jerry Lester, Milton Delugg, and Dagmar.

increasing competition from a slew of similarly structured talk shows. This continued with Johnny Carson's reign, and yet all of the competing programs were content to stick to the same talk show format, without an interest in adopting the more variety-style presentation of *Broadway Open House*.

In late 1971, Richard Doan lamented in *TV Guide*, "Is there nothing new for late-night TV? It seems that way. All three networks air 'desk-and-sofa shows' whose main difference is that they are presided over by different individuals. CBS, frustrated in its belated attempt to compete with NBC's long-established *Tonight Show*, has been scrounging about for something different to replace Merv Griffin's show." Doan suggested what, to him, was an obvious answer: "Late-show movies or a *Broadway Open House*-type variety show, perhaps with a different host each night. Both ideas have at least one thing going for them—they were hot 20 years ago." Alas, little changed within the genre for the next twenty years, either.

The first feature film ever shown on television

It isn't so easy to single out the first feature film ever to air on TV. Each of the following choices can suitably serve as the "correct" one, so it's all really in the eye of the beholder. But, as mentioned earlier, some examples relate more to the experimental years of television, when short-range transmissions took place more for the benefit of broadcast engineers than for the few private citizens who had the means to receive TV signals at home.

A brief news item in the *New York Times* in December 1928 claimed that the Chicago radio station WCFL, owned by the Chicago Federation of Labor, and active in experimenting with television (to the tune of about $100,000 that year), had successfully transmitted motion pictures. Chief Engineer Virgil A. Schoenberg said the movies were "the same kind as those shown in theatres." Representatives of RCA were reportedly present during the demonstration, but the films themselves were not identified by name.

In 1929, Philo Farnsworth experimented with broadcasting a motion picture when he chose an excerpt of *The Taming of the Shrew*, starring Mary Pickford and Douglas Fairbanks, released that same year.

Television historian Patrick Robertson cites "the first full-length feature film shown on television was *Police Patrol* (1925), transmitted in six daily episodes by DuMont's W2XCD, Passaic, New Jersey, April 6-11, 1931."

Film director Michael Ritchie, who authored an excellent pre-history of television titled *Stay Tuned*, cites Don Lee's experimental TV station W6XAO in Los Angeles as "the first broadcasting station to show a current full-length motion picture, *The Crooked Circle*." This was followed by Gary Cooper in *The Texan*. Ritchie doesn't supply a date for the broadcast, but it was probably in 1933.

In 1938, NBC in New York aired the film *The Return of the Scarlet Pimpernel*. As it was reported the following day, "A full-length movie, running nearly an hour and a half, went on the television airways last night. Listeners and lookers-in over a radius of more than forty miles from middle Manhattan followed the dramatic action of Alexander Korda's production." The film was carried by special coaxial cable to the Empire State Building's television transmitter, where it was broadcast, coupled onto radio waves to the receivers scattered through the metropolitan area.

Some invited guests viewed the show on a television in the NBC board room in Radio City, while another group watched in the Mecca Temple on West Fifty-sixth Street. And, just to make sure the signal was reaching real TV homes in the area, fifty to seventy-five engineers and observers viewed the show at their homes in Manhattan, Long Island and Westchester, before reporting back to NBC.

The network touted it as the first full-length film ever to be televised in the nation, and went on to explain that this particular production "was selected to ascertain if pictures of this type are good program material, and if such shows will hold the attention of the audience for an hour and a half." An oft-repeated story tells of the projectionist getting the order of the reels mixed up and playing the last reel before he was supposed to, thus ending the film almost twenty minutes early. And, supposedly, no Hollywood films were sold to NBC for another decade due to that blunder. However, the mishap was not mentioned in either *The New York Times* or *Broadcasting* magazine's reported accounts of the broadcast.

In 1941, the first year of FCC-approved commercial television, New York's NBC station's broadcast of the RKO film *Millionaire Playboy* was interrupted by a news bulletin announcing the Japanese bombing of Pearl Harbor (more about that later).

In the mid-1940s, some stations began running silent Westerns and other low-budget shorts as time fillers in their schedules. In 1948, local New York station WPIX acquired the rights from British producer Sir Alexander Korda to run twenty-four British dramas. As for American films, Hollywood producers began to loosen their grip on films produced before 1948, so they could air on TV without being in direct competition with those still being run in theaters.

In 1957, *Hollywood Film Theater* on ABC began running some of the more successful films of the 1930s and 1940s. But it wasn't until NBC instituted *Saturday Night at the Movies* in 1961 that contemporary films of the time began appearing regularly on TV.

The first made-for-TV movie

In 1944, the newly-formed RKO Television Productions filmed the one-hour drama *Talk Fast, Mister* at the RKO-Pathe Studios in New York. It was produced in arrangement with DuMont, which aired it that December, making it the first film made especially for television.

In the post-war era, the premiere episode of NBC's anthology series *Your Show Time* aired in January 1948, with a filmed production of "The Necklace," based on a Guy de Maupassant story. It won the first-ever Emmy Award for an original TV production, but at a half-hour running time, it obviously could not be considered a feature-length movie.

The 1957 film *The Pied Piper of Hamelin*, a family musical starring Van Johnson, is sometimes cited as the first TV movie. Based on the poem by Robert Browning, the film at the very least holds the distinction of being the first *color* feature-length film shot for TV. It aired on NBC on November 26, 1957.

In the early 1960s, as theatrical films found a growing audience on television, the networks placed a heavy demand on the supply from the major studios. Eventually, films were commissioned specifically for TV broadcast rather than for release in movie theaters. The first of these, *See How They Run,* debuted on NBC on October 7, 1964 (an earlier production, *The Killers,* was deemed too violent for TV, and was released theatrically).

Over time, made-for-TV movies continued to strengthen their foothold on the network schedules, so much so that in the fall of 1969, perennial third-place network ABC introduced *The Movie of the Week* on Tuesday nights. The classic opening sequence featured state-of-the-art graphics and visual effects, a soaring musical theme by Burt Bacharach, and a voiceover announcing, "The Movie of the Week—presenting the world premiere of an original motion picture produced especially for ABC." In 1971, an additional *Movie of the Week* installment was added on Saturday nights (later moving to Wednesdays).

Among the more memorable entries in the *Movie of the Week* history were: *Duel,* starring Dennis Weaver and directed by rookie Steven Spielberg; *Brian's Song,* a memorable tearjerker and winner of five Emmys; and the aptly-named *Trilogy of Terror,* written by the legendary sci-fi writer Richard Matheson, featuring a memorable and horrifying story of a tiny but homicidal African Zuni doll running amuck in a young woman's apartment. *Movie of the Week* also aired several pilots for future weekly series, such as *The Six Million Dollar Man, Starsky and Hutch,* and *Marcus Welby, M.D.*

The Movie of the Week became such a staple in prime time that, even decades after it formally left the air, actors plugging their new television projects on talk shows could still be caught speaking of their upcoming roles in a " movie-of-the-week," thus turning the title into more of a generic label.

One of the most controversial made-for-TV films in history, *The Day After,* aired on November 20, 1983, with an estimated 100 million viewers— the largest audience for a TV movie to this day (a 46.0 rating and 62 share). The film, with a large cast headed by Jason Robards, dramatized the idea of the United States plunging into a war with the Soviet Union, resulting in a nuclear exchange. The main focus of the story follows the victims of an atomic bomb attack near Lawrence, Kansas.The film and its disturbing scenario became a hot topic of debate throughout the media in the days before, during, and after the broadcast.

The first TV series based on a feature film

Dating back to the earliest days of network television, almost 200 series have aired as adaptations of feature films. The vast majority of these experienced only a short stay on the tube, while others (*M*A*S*H*, *The Odd Couple*, *Buffy the Vampire Slayer*) managed to match or exceed the popularity of the films on which they were based.

The very first television program based on a feature film was *The Front Page*, adapted from the classic 1928 newsroom stage play by Ben Hecht and Charles MacArthur. The comedy was a Broadway hit, prompting a 1931 film version, and later a 1940 film version—renamed *His Girl Friday*, starring Cary Grant and Rosalind Russell. *The Front Page* as a TV series premiered in the fall of 1949. As *Television* magazine assessed the new incarnation, "*The Front Page* should make for highly entertaining series providing the producer doesn't work to death Hildy Johnson's quitting in every program. The show was well produced and cast except for Walter Burns. John Daly is just a bit too smooth and somehow doesn't measure up to the original conception of the Hecht-MacArthur perennial." The program lasted only four months.

The first TV series to be made *into* a feature film

There have been over thirty prime time television series that, after leaving the airwaves, were given new life as feature films. But the track record has been mixed. While some action series have fared well on the big screen, most notably *Star Trek*, *Batman*, *Mission: Impossible*, and *Charlie's Angels*, sitcom adaptations have resulted in mostly cringe-worthy commercial and critical failures.

The Goldbergs began life on radio and found a home on TV in 1949, to great success. In March of 1951, *Molly*, a film version of the series, opened to favorable reviews, making it the first prime time TV series to be made into a feature film—even as it continued its run as a weekly program. The *New York Times* promised that "a visit to the Paramount Theatres, where *Molly* was presented yesterday, should leave every good neighbor in a happy frame of mind . . . There is uncommon warmth and naturalness in each of [the actors'] performances, but Mrs. Berg understandably is the center of attention and delight."

In late December of 1951, television's first sci-fi series, *Captain Video*, premiered as a serial in movie theaters, two seasons into the program's TV run. Columbia Pictures produced *Captain Video: Master of the Stratosphere* as a 15-chapter series, featuring a different cast than that of the TV program, but it proved quite successful.

Thanks to the tremendous success of *Dragnet* upon its television premiere in 1952, a feature film version was produced and released in 1954, starring series creator/producer/star Jack Webb, and his onscreen partner Ben Alexander as Frank Smith. The plot had Friday and Smith investigating the shooting of a small-time hood by a big-time organized crime boss. The film's other stars included Dennis Weaver as the District Attorney, and Richard Boone as Friday's boss.

A few more early examples of television series moving on to movie screens include the slapstick military sitcom *McHale's Navy*, which ran on ABC from 1962 to 1966. Halfway through its run, in June 1964, Universal released the *McHale's Navy* feature film, starring the cast from the series, including Ernest Borgnine, Joe Flynn, and Tim Conway (a follow-up film, *McHale's Navy Joins the Air Force*, did not include Borgnine).

In May of 1966, *The Munsters* was canceled after two seasons on the air, but only a month later, *Munster Go Home* opened in theaters. It was a color feature film that took the spooky family overseas to meet their relatives in England.

Interestingly, most television series that have been adapted as feature films didn't make it onto movie theater screens until many years, even decades, after they last aired on TV. The nostalgia factor, somewhat cynically employed by film studios to appeal to the maturing baby-boomer generation, has been in large part to blame. Most of these feature film adaptations have been of sitcoms, including *Sgt. Bilko, Car 54, Where Are You?, The Honeymooners* (with a black cast), *Bewitched,* and the live-action version of *The Flintstones.* Despite the generally disappointing results, the practice continued into the new millennium, with *The X-Files, Veronica Mars* and comedies such as *South Park,* and *Reno 911* making the jump from small to big screen.

The first spinoff

The spinoff is sort of the duck-billed platypus of the television kingdom. While it can certainly be considered its own category of TV program, it also can derive from a number of differing sources. Most spinoff series are created by taking a popular character from an original series and creating a pilot episode to set up that character in his or her own new series. Sometimes a character remains in the same locale as the original, allowing for crossover episodes or guest appearances by others from the original. Sometimes a character is transplanted to a new setting. In still other instances, the locale remains the same, but is re-populated with a totally new set of characters.

Wanted: Dead Or Alive, part of the avalanche of westerns dominating television in the late 1950s, starred Steve McQueen as bounty hunter Josh Randall in a March 1958 episode of the series *Trackdown*, which starred Robert Culp as a Texas Ranger. *Wanted: Dead Or Alive* began its regular run in later that same year, making it network television's first spinoff. However—and here's where it gets a little tricky—*Trackdown* itself first aired in May of 1957 as a stand-alone episode of *Dick Powell's Zane Grey Theater*, an anthology series of tales from the Old West, based on books written by Zane Grey and other authors. But it's doubtful that *Trackdown* can be considered a true spinoff, since *Zane Grey Theater*, by definition, did not have a regular setting or set of characters from week to week.

The first program to be revived after its initial run

Just as there have been a good many TV series to make the hit-or-miss leap into feature films, many others have been given a second life of first-run episodes, either on a network or in syndication, after their initial run. Some have reunited part or all of their original casts, while others were re-built almost from scratch, retaining little more than the title and/or original premise. Some fared quite well in their second life, while others disappeared quickly without being noticed (several game shows, such as *Can You Top This? Concentration, Jeopardy,* and *You Bet Your Life* have all been revived at least once through the decades, with mixed success, but here we'll focus on prime time scripted series).

The first network program to re-appear on TV screens after the conclusion of its initial run was *The Life of Riley*. This early sitcom, first made popular on radio with William Bendix in the lead, debuted on NBC in October 1949, starring Jackie Gleason as Riley (Bendix had too many movie commitments to continue the series on television). The show lasted until its cancellation in March 1950, but was revived in January 1953, with Bendix back in the lead, along with an entirely new cast. The program enjoyed another five years on the air, ending in August of 1958.

The following is a purely random selection of prime time dramas and sitcoms that were resurrected after the conclusion of their original runs.

Dragnet – This classic and much parodied police series, created and produced by Jack Webb, originated on radio in 1949 and continued on television beginning in 1952, where it ran a solid five seasons. In 1967 it accomplished the then-rare feat of returning for a new four-season run, this time with Harry Morgan playing Friday's partner, Bill Gannon. This new *Dragnet,* in its earnest attempt to keep up with the times, dealt with 1960s issues such as the counter-culture, drug abuse, and hippies, who often gave Friday and Gannon fits of frustration. Reruns of this incarnation have long been a common staple in syndication and, in recent years, on nostalgia-heavy cable networks.

In 1989, yet another version of *Dragnet* appeared, produced for syndication and yielding fifty-two episodes. While the storytelling style for the new *Dragnet* remained faithful to Webb's versions, Joe Friday and his supporting characters were replaced (!) by a new team of L.A.'s finest.

Perry Mason – Legendary defense attorney Perry Mason, created in a series of books by Erle Stanley Gardner, first starred in six feature films produced between 1934 and 1937. He came to TV in 1957, with Raymond Burr in the title role (the original choice for the part: Fred MacMurray). Mason, aided by secretary Della Street and private investigator Paul Drake, set the standard for the many later courtroom dramas, even though the series' often-used gimmick—the last-minute outburst by the guilty party watching from the back of the courtroom—was hardly television's most realistic depiction of the American legal process.

The series ended in 1966. It was revived briefly in 1973, as *The New Adventures of Perry Mason*, with Monte Markham in the lead (Raymond Burr was starring in *Ironside* at the time), but the series had only a brief run. In 1985, Burr returned to the role (along with Barbara Hale as Della Street) in a series of TV movies, which aired a few times a year until Burr's death in 1993.

The Twilight Zone – created by Rod Serling, this anthology of stories, ranging from humorous to terrifying (but each including a surprising twist ending) remains among the top ten classic TV series of all time. It ran for five seasons. In 1983, an attempt to adapt a few of the series' original episodes as self-contained segments of a single feature film met with mixed reviews. (While filming a newly-written story for the movie, actor Vic Morrow and two other actors were killed on the set by a pyrotechnic malfunction, causing a helicopter to fall on top of them.)

In 1985, a decade after Serling's death, CBS resurrected *The Twilight Zone* as a one-hour series, with each episode containing two or three stories. Most were new, some were re-makes from the original. In 1987 the series continued in syndication, once again as a half-hour show, with thirty new episodes added to those from the CBS seasons.

In 2002, the series was brought back yet again, with actor Forest Whitaker as host. It aired on the UPN network for forty-four episodes, some of which were updated versions of those from the original series.

The Munsters – The original horror film spoof sitcom *The Munsters* premiered in September 1964, as part of a wave of fantasy comedies that included *The Addams Family, Bewitched*, the much-maligned *My Mother the Car*, and, beginning the following season, *I Dream of Jeannie*.

The Munsters was canceled at the end of the 1965-66 season. Twenty-two years later, in October of 1988, an updated version of the program returned in syndication as *The Munsters Today*. An all-new cast included John Schuck as Herman and Lee Meriwether as Lilly. While it was not considered a great creative success, lacking the charm and originality of the first series, it did live on for seventy-two episodes, a shade over the original series' total.

Gidget – This sitcom, following the life of energetic California surfer Frances "Gidget" Lawrence, lasted a single season as a TV show in 1965-66, after which the Gidget character returned to the feature films from whence she came. In 1986, a syndicated revival of the show—with an entirely different cast and titled *The New Gidget*—caught up with Gidget, now in her late twenties, married, and running her own travel agency. Her teenage niece caused most of the trouble along the lines Gidget herself created in the original series. *The New Gidget* ran for forty-four episodes.

Mission: Impossible – This innovative CBS spy show originally starred Steven Hill, and later Peter Graves (who would be forever identified with the series), and deliberately placed its emphasis on action, intricate plots, and impressive gadgetry—including self-destructing audio tapes—rather than much in the way of character development among the leads. The IMF (Impossible Mission Force) specialized in foiling the evil plans of various small-time dictators, crime lords, and spies from hostile nations. The series ran from September 1966 to June 1973.

The series was revived in 1988, due partly to the Hollywood writer's strike, which left production companies with a dearth of new scripts and series to develop and get on the air. ABC decided to bring back the show with its familiar format (the self-destructing tapes were updated to small video disks). The new version was filmed in Australia, with Graves again in the lead, but with a new supporting cast, including Phil Morris, son of original cast member Greg Morris, and Jane Badler (the villainess of *V*).The show lasted two seasons.

Star Trek – The original *Star Trek* series ran for three seasons between 1966 and 1969, but throughout the 1970s and 1980s its popularity as a cult favorite only grew, thanks to the program's syndicated reruns and string of feature films. The series was resurrected in 1987 with the arrival of *Star Trek: The Next Generation,* and the subsequent series *Star Trek: Deep Space Nine, Star Trek: Voyager, and Star Trek: Enterprise.*

This begs the question: When is a spinoff not a spinoff, but more of a "sequel," if it's without the original series' cast of characters? In the case of *Star Trek*, it's pretty much a matter of semantics. While the characters of the original series did not return in the later television incarnations (with a few rare exceptions, made possible by the wonders of science fiction), the Enterprise, in refurbished form, remained, as did other elements and back-stories. The success of *The Next Generation* allowed the *Star Trek* franchise to thrive for years.

Later series to follow this model of launching related versions as part of a series "brand" have included *Law and Order* and its spin-offs, and the C.S.I. franchise.

Ironside – Just a year after ending his nine season stint as Perry Mason, Raymond Burr began what would become an eight year run as San Francisco Chief of Detectives Robert Ironside, confined to a wheelchair after surviving an assassination attempt. In September of 2013, a new version of the series premiered, starring Blair Underwood, but viewers did not accept him as Ironside. NBC cancelled the series due to low ratings, after airing just two episodes.

The Fugitive – This was one of the most popular drama series of the mid-1960s, as its storyline followed Dr. Richard Kimble, mistakenly but doggedly pursued by the law (in the person of Lieutenant Gerard) for the murder of his wife. While on the run, Kimble also sought to find the real murderer, a one-armed man he happened to glimpse fleeing the scene of the crime.

After its hugely successful 1967 finale, seen by a record-breaking number of viewers, and a 1993 feature film version starring Harrison Ford, the series was revived on TV in 2000, with Tim Daly in the lead, but the new version lasted only a single season.

Hawaii Five-O – The exotic locale and driving theme music contributed to the uniqueness of this police series, filmed in Honolulu, starring Jack Lord (and co-starring his pompadour hairstyle). It ran from 1968 to 1980. The show returned on CBS in an updated form on September 20, 2010, exactly 42 years to the day of the original version's premiere episode, with Alex O'Laughlin as Steve McGarrett. This new version reached its 100th episode milestone in 2014, a rare feat for a revived series.

Rowan and Martin's Laugh-In – Those of a certain age will fondly remember this landmark sketch comedy show, created and produced by George Schlatter, which premiered in 1968 and kept up its frenetic pace until its cancellation 1973. In 1977, Schlatter brought it back as a series of monthly specials, simply titled *Laugh-In '77*, with a brand new cast of young comedians—but without Rowan and Martin. In fact, the comedy team brought a lawsuit against Schlatter for reviving the series without their permission. It was hardly worth their effort, as lightning failed to strike twice. Only six episodes aired. Viewing audiences were unimpressed by the unknowns in the cast—except for a young Robin Williams. When Williams hit the big time in *Mork & Mindy* the following season, the *Laugh-In* specials were rerun to capitalize on his new-found fame.

Columbo – This truly distinctive detective series, starring Peter Falk as the rumpled, disorganized, but brilliant Lieutenant Columbo, was one of the few programs in TV history that voluntarily ended its original run (1971-78) while still maintaining the high quality of writing and acting for which it had become so popular. It originally rotated with other series (including *McCloud* and *McMillan & Wife*) as part of the *NBC Sunday Mystery Movie*. After production on *Columbo* shut down in 1978, rumors made the rounds every so often speculating whether Falk might be persuaded to return to the role. Falk had never ruled it out, and in fact always professed his enjoyment playing the character. Finally, in 1989, ABC brought back *Columbo* as a series of TV movies, with the original series co-creator William Link as producer. The new episodes aired irregularly until the final installment in 2004.

The Bionic Woman – A classic sci-fi cult favorite, spun off from the series *The Six Million Dollar Man* (based on the Martin Caidin novel *Cyborg*), *The Bionic Woman* premiered in January 1976 on ABC, but in September 1977, it continued its run for a final season on NBC. And, while the show incorporated its fair share of now-cheesy special effects and stock villains, its selling point was always the charm and beauty of star Lindsay Wagner as Jaime Sommers.

The series was revived in September 2007, with British actress Michelle Ryan cast as Jaime. While Ryan had achieved considerable success on British

TV in the staggeringly popular nighttime soap *Eastenders*, she had to adopt an American accent for her role as Jaime, which seemed to put a damper on her otherwise solid acting abilities. The revival stumbled through its first few episodes, as critics pounced and fans loyal to the original series rebelled.

Peter Falk as *Columbo*.

The show began to gain its creative footing just as an industry-wide Writer's Guild strike interrupted production in November. Only the first eight episodes of the remake had aired. But once the strike was settled, *The Bionic Woman* did not reappear. At first, NBC denied that the show had been cancelled, but the network also didn't air any remaining episodes, or order new ones. With poor ratings and heavy criticism of the reboot, it was determined that continuing production would become more trouble than it was worth.

Dallas – One of the most popular prime time soap operas in history, *Dallas* originally ran from April 1978 to May 1991, securing its lofty place in TV history. In June 2012, TNT revived the series, with many of the original cast returning, including Larry Hagman as J.R. Ewing, Patrick Duffy as Bobby Ewing, and Linda Gray as J.R.'s wife, Sue Ellen. The storyline picked up right where it left off eleven years earlier. Larry Hagman died of cancer in November of that same year, but despite his death—and the death of J.R.—the show continued, until its cancellation in September 2014.

Cagney & Lacey – This series presented the team of two women police detectives (the first such team on TV), chasing bad guys and solving crimes in New York. The original TV-movie aired in October 1981, starring Loretta Swit as Christine Cagney, and Tyne Daly as Mary Beth Lacey. When the series premiered in March 1982 for a six episode run, Meg Foster took over as Cagney. Good reviews but poor ratings (and murmurings that the two leads were not feminine enough) led to cancellation. When producer Barney Rosenzweig secured Sharon Gless (his future wife) to play Cagney, CBS agreed to give the show another chance, the series was given a slot on the 1982-83 schedule.

But the series was canceled a second time, in May of 1983, at which point Rosenzweig organized a letter-writing campaign among the show's fans, who were modest in number but passionate in their support for the program. This, in addition to a change in time slots for summer reruns, plus an Emmy nomination for Tyne Daly (which she won), brought strong ratings for the presumed-dead series.

Consequently, the series returned yet again, as a mid-season replacement in March 1984. From that point through the rest of its run, *Cagney &*

Lacey garnered thirty-six Emmy nominations and fourteen wins, including two for Best Drama Series, four Best Actress awards for Tyne Day, and two for Sharon Gless.

At the end of the seventh season, stiff competition and a big ratings slide forced CBS to cancel the show for the third and final time.

V – This series began as a two-part miniseries on NBC in 1984, telling the sci-fi tale of an alien race coming to Earth announcing its good intentions. But *V* was actually a thinly-disguised parallel to the rise of Nazi Germany (the "V" being part of the Rebellion's motto, "V for Victory"). A sequel, *V: The Final Battle*, followed, and *V* began a regular series for the 1984-85 season.

In November 2009, amid much hype, the series was re-made and began a new life on ABC, but was met with so-so reviews and mediocre ratings. It ran until March 2011.

Beverly Hills 90210 – Beginning in October of 1990, this teen drama on the Fox network centered on wealthy and considerably spoiled high schoolers (with the exception of main characters Brandon and Brenda Walsh, who moved with their middle-class parents to Beverly Hills from Minnesota) and enjoyed staggering popularity with the younger demographic audience. The show survived numerous cast changes throughout its ten year run. Eight years after it concluded, the CW network brought the series back as simply *90210*, with a new cast of high schoolers, but also with multi-episode guest appearances by original stars Shannon Dougherty and Jennie Garth, reprising their roles as Brenda and her best friend Kellie. The re-make version ran five seasons, before its final episode aired in February 2013.

Arrested Development – This quirky, single-camera sitcom, following the exploits of the eccentric Bluth family (whose patriarch had been serving prison time) ran on the Fox network for three seasons, between 2003 and 2006, and gained an intense following.

In 2013, an arrangement brought back the series, with the original cast, for a ten episode run on Netflix.

24 – One of television's most innovative spy-intrigue series, *24* premiered in November 2001, and centered on agent Jack Bauer of the U.S. Government's Counter-Terrorism Unit (Kiefer Sutherland). The storyline unfolded in real time, i.e. each one-hour episode paralleled exactly one hour in the series' 24-hour timeline (a digital clock intermittently displayed in the corner of the screen made sure to remind viewers of the fact).

The series ended in May 2010 after eight seasons and 192 episodes, but Sutherland and his co-producers teased fans with hints of a possible feature film version. When that idea failed to pan out, it was then decided to return the series to network TV. In the 2013-14 season, *24: Live Another Day* ran as limited run of twelve one-hour episodes.

The first program to run twenty consecutive years on television

In November of 1947, the public affairs discussion program *Meet the Press* first aired as a local program in Washington, D.C. on the NBC affiliate. Two weeks later, it continued as a network show when WNBT in New York carried the broadcast as well. At that time, the show was a prime time program, and, in 1951, began airing twice a week. In August 1965, it became a weekly staple on Sunday mornings. In 1967, *Meet the Press* marked its 20th consecutive year on the air, the first American television program of any kind to do so. Of course, it has since celebrated its 30th, 40th, 50th, and 60th anniversaries.

The first program to run twenty consecutive years in prime time was *The Ed Sullivan Show* (originally titled *The Toast of the Town*). Sullivan's Sunday evening variety show premiered on June 20, 1948, and continued for twenty-three years until its cancellation in June 1971. *The Original Amateur Hour* hosted by Ted Mack, could be considered a close runner-up. That program, originally popular on radio and featuring an array of show business hopefuls presenting their talents, debuted on the DuMont network on January 18, 1948, and ran with just a few gaps for the next twenty-two years on NBC and ABC. *The Red Skelton Show* is another early program that ran for twenty straight years, between 1951 and 1971.

As for prime time dramas, *Gunsmoke* was the first to run twenty

Ed Sullivan formally introduced the Beatles to seventy-three million viewers in February of 1964, during his program's sixteenth season.

consecutive seasons, from 1955 to 1975, with James Arness as Matt Dillon leading the cast for the entire run.

Law & Order matched that twenty year span in its final season. The legal drama premiered in September 1990 and ended its run in May 2010, after filming a total of 456 episodes (in comparison, *Gunsmoke* filmed 635 episodes throughout its twenty year run).

There is a prime time program still on the air that has been seen weekly for over *four* straight decades, since its debut in 1968. That program is *60 Minutes*.

However, we'd be remiss not to acknowledge the all-time champion for longevity. It was not a prime time program, but rather a daytime soap opera. *The Guiding Light* premiered on radio for CBS on January 25, 1937, and, after fifteen years, continued on television beginning on June 30, 1952, where it remained on the air for the next fifty-seven years, until its cancellation in September 2009—making for a total lifespan of seventy-two years!

CHAPTER 3
THE TECHNOLOGICAL FIRSTS

The first live TV broadcast transmitted overseas

There is a long-forgotten but astonishing fact that a signal carrying a live television picture crossed the Atlantic for the first time not in 1962, with the help of the new Telstar satellite, but as early as February 8, 1928. Once again, the Father of Television, John Logie Baird, was responsible for the accomplishment, adding yet another milestone to his impressive list of television firsts.

Baird painstakingly prepared for the experiment to transmit a television signal from England to the United States, culminating in the early hours of February 9 (London time). There, in his lab, a small group of guest witnesses gathered to watch the transmission.

On the American side, preparations were made to pick up the signal at an amateur receiving station in Hartsdale, New York. Those present were Capt. O.G. Hutchinson, the Joint Managing Director of the Baird Company; Mr. Clapp, one of the company's engineers; Mr. Hart, the owner of the amateur wireless station; and the Reuter's press representative.

Upon initiating the transmission (which used a mere two kilowatts of power), Baird gave the witnesses at the New York end an opportunity to adjust the receiving apparatus. After amplification, the signal was then applied to the receiving televisor, consisting of a ground glass screen measuring about two inches by three inches. The image of Baird's Stooky Bill doll was transmitted first. The image was accompanied by a sound "which sounded for all the world like the drone of a huge bee," as it was sent over a telephone line first to the Baird company's private experimental wireless station at Coulsdon. From there, the image was flashed across the Atlantic.

When the image of the doll's head had been satisfactorily tuned in, Hart started up his own transmitter and called a receiving station operator at Purley, near London. His message to Baird was to ask the inventor to sit in front of the transmitter, replacing the doll. This message was telephoned from the Purley receiving station to the laboratories at Long Acre.

Baird sat before the transmitter for a half hour, moving his head in different directions, until the message came through from New York that his image had come through clearly. The report from the receiving end described how "the vision of the man on the London end came through in a form suggestive of a Jack-o-lantern, but a Jack-o-lantern that could turn its head from side to side and open its mouth. A newspaper reporter named Fox then took Baird's place, and continued to sit before the televisor until word came through that his image had come though quite well. It was later reported that "Mr. Fox's features were particularly striking, from a television point of view, and transmitted better than those of other sitters."

The wife of another journalist present then took a turn to have her image transmitted, although her features were not as recognizable at the American end. "The vision of the woman appeared broken and scattered, but it still was plain that she was a woman and that she was showing first the full face and then the profile."

Those assembled at the London were able to see, on a check receiver, a pilot image of what was being transmitted. This enabled the transmitting operator to check the outgoing transmission and correct any irregularities.

This full-size image showed only the head of each sitter, with the complete details of their features showing in black relief on an orange-colored background. Atmospheric interference and a fading signal disrupted the incoming image in Hartsdale at times, "but in spite of these disabilities, reception was, on the whole, very good. The demonstration proved quite conclusively that if a much higher powered wireless transmitter had been employed, the image would have been received in New York entirely free from atmospheric and other disturbances. An important feature is that only two operators were required to attend to the television transmission, one at each end of the circuit."

Upon reporting the news of the successful experiment, *The New York Times* declared that "Man's vision had spanned the ocean; transatlantic television was a demonstrated reality, and one more great dream of science was on the way to realization."

The same paper also printed an editorial which was quick to praise Baird and predicted great things for television. "His images were crude; they were scarcely recognizable; they faded and reappeared as the atmospheric conditions varied; but they were the beginnings of a new branch of engineering which is destined to convert the earth into something like a planetary motion picture house in which whole populations will follow flickering reproductions of remotely occurring events on a screen."

As the British magazine *Television* reported in its first issue:

"At the beginning of this year, the record distance over which television had been publicly demonstrated was between London and Glasgow, by Mr. J.L. Baird. To transmit vision over such a distance—435 miles—seemed at the time to be a most phenomenal achievement; yet, just after we had gone to press with this issue there burst upon the world the startling news that the Atlantic had been spanned by television! Again by Mr. Baird! Just what does this mean? It means that recognizable images of human beings seated in the heart of London were seen in New York, over 3,500 miles away!"

This success occurred only three weeks after GE engineers had been patting each other on the back for transmitting an over-the-air TV image from their Schenectady lab out to receiver sets within a 20-mile radius.

A decade after Baird's experiment, another—but unexpected—overseas transmission reached America's east coast from England. For a period in 1938, a burst of sunspot activity had a great effect on transmission signals reaching the ionosphere. Television transmissions sent out from the BBC's studios in Alexandra Palace in London normally reached a 30-mile radius, but at one point, the atmospheric conditions enabled the TV signals to bounce off the ionosphere and reach across the Atlantic. RCA engineers in New York quickly took advantage of the phenomena and proceeded to film the incoming images off of one of their receiving monitors. The shaky and mostly distorted pictures stabilized long enough to make it possible to later identify the on-air BBC personalities Jasmine Bligh and Elizabeth Cowell, separately addressing the camera. Also visible was a scene featuring actors performing in a period costume drama. The film by the RCA engineers thus became the first kinescope in history (nine years before the networks officially instituted their own systems), but the film then vanished for the next several decades. Attempts by television historians to track it down were unsuccessful, until British researcher Andrew Emmerson found former RCA employee Maurice Schechter in the 1990s. Schechter had a number of 16mm films in his possession containing various early broadcast material. As Emmerson told the London *Times* in 1999, "He cleaned it up digitally and transferred it to a video cassette for me. I was astounded. This was the oldest and probably the only example of live high-definition television from the pre-war period."

The first all-electronic television set sold to the public

In the earliest years of television's existence, it became popular for radio enthusiasts, who wanted to get in on television's ground floor, to buy crude adaptors that, when hooked up to their radio receivers, could also pick up over-the-air experimental TV signals onto a small screen.

By 1938, television signals were being sent and received solely by electronic means. And, while television's "official" launch at the 1939 New York World's Fair was still a year away, progress had already reached the point whereby Allen DuMont's TV manufacturing company was able to put the first all-electronic TV receiver on the market. The Model 180, with an 8" x 10" picture tube, was nicknamed the "Clifton," after the New Jersey town in which the company was based.

The first cable TV system

With cable television as prevalent as it is throughout the U.S., and run by perpetually-merging mega-conglomerates, it's easy to forget that the original concept of cable TV was to help over-the-air signals reach households in mountainous regions of the country, where reception was poor. Originally referred to as Community Antenna Television (CATV), the first cable TV system was developed in 1948, in the Mahanoy City region of Pennsylvania.

John and Margaret Walson had formed the Service Electric Company in the mid-1940s to sell and service General Electric appliances. Shortly after they began selling television sets in 1947, they heard of problems about poor reception from many of their customers. John had already attached an antenna to a utility pole on a local mountain top, and connected it to his store via a cable and signal boosters, which enabled him to successfully demonstrate his TVs with signals from the three Philadelphia network affiliates. In June of 1948, he connected the cable to a few of his customers' homes, thus creating the first small, crude cable TV system.

In 1970, 4.5 million households were plugged into cable. In 1980, there were 17 million. However, by the *end* of the 1980s, the number had exploded to 52 million households and 79 cable networks.

The first use of kinescopes on broadcast television

At the dawn of television broadcasting, there was no dependable way to create a permanent audio/visual record of anything being transmitted over the airwaves, even though experiments had been conducted since the late 1920s to record, on film or by other means, over-the-air television transmissions.

True, the earliest of broadcasts were reaching precious few private homes around the country, and mostly in major cities like New York, Chicago, and Los Angeles. But it wasn't until the late 1940s when TV programs could be preserved for posterity. The arrival of the kinescope, a mechanical unit created basically by pointing a film camera at a studio monitor as a television program aired live, was officially announced on September 13, 1947. It was the result of a joint project between Kodak, NBC, and DuMont. The first kinescope unit was unveiled at an NBC affiliates convention in Atlantic City, New Jersey.

The process worked like this: after a live program was televised, and recorded off a kinescope monitor onto film, the film was then processed, and copies were physically shipped to TV stations elsewhere in the country, to air at times of their own discretion. It was an inexpensive and relatively simple way of strengthening the concept of a true TV network among stations dotted across the country. And, while it was a somewhat crude method, the kinescope helped preserve countless classic (and not-so-classic) live TV broadcasts throughout the late 1940s and early 1950s.

But the kinescope picture quality was a frequent source of complaint by station managers, television critics, and viewers. *Television* magazine, in its August 1949 issue, pointed out both the advantages and disadvantages of kinescopes: "Undoubtedly one of the most important developments in TV is film recordings, variously referred to as kinescope recordings, video transcriptions and Tele Transcriptions, etc., etc. The importance of film recording is emphasized by the fact that approximately 30 hours of this type of programming is turned out each week by the four networks, and that some 30 advertisers are placing recordings on 49 individual stations."

As for the disadvantages, kinescopes were inferior to producing a program directly on to film, and the kinescope images were at the mercy of the image quality appearing on the studio recording monitor. *Television* went on to explain that "the generally short rehearsal time, inadequate studio facilities, the necessity for continuous action without an opportunity for retakes, and dissimilarity of television camera characteristics tremendously complicate the production of a program. Thus the image to be recorded may and does vary over a wide range of quality."

A few months later, *Televiser* magazine grumbled, "A mediocre or poor recording is not worth telecasting. The lighting fades and flickers, the performers look like they have been recently disinterred. It is an unfortunate fact that most kinescope recordings seen on the air fall into this group. Simply turn on your set and watch almost any one of the thirty odd TV programs now being telecast by film recordings. And you better wear dark glasses to prevent snow blindness." But the piece also conceded that, "at the present time there is no other method available."

The first TV series produced on film

The frustration with kinescope quality spurred many in the industry to come up with alternative methods. In 1947, film director Jerry Fairbanks dove into television by filming twenty-six episodes of a new crime drama, *Public Prosecutor*. NBC planned to air the series, but later reneged on the deal when Fairbanks delivered 20-minute episodes, instead of half-hour episodes.

In January 1948, NBC replaced *Public Prosecutor* on its schedule with the drama anthology *Your Show Time*, the first television series on the air to film its episodes, rather than present them live and/or kinescoped. Each week, series' host Arthur Shields introduced a different half-hour filmed adaptation of a short story, usually by a famous author such as Robert Louis Stevenson, Mark Twain, or Sir Arthur Conan Doyle.

Shortly thereafter, Fairbanks went on to make a far greater contribution to television: a new, multi-camera film system, combining both TV and film shooting techniques. It permitted a program to be filmed in continuous action, cutting from one camera to another, thus greatly reducing production time.

"The new technique developed in our research laboratories," Fairbanks explained, "utilizes three or more 16mm Mitchell cameras which can operate simultaneously, filming three or more different angles of a scene and getting long, medium and close-up shots at the same time. The procedure is similar to the use of three cameras in telecasting 'live' videos. Heretofore, separate film camera set-ups have been used for the same results."

After comparing his sample reel footage favorably over kinescope footage several times, Fairbanks went on to boast of this method's superior picture quality, lighting, and sound over kinescopes.

> The difference in our opinion is startling, especially when seen on a closed circuit. This new method of making TV film does away with all the objectionable features of kinescopes and makes it

possible for a star to do an entire series in a short period of time, thereby freeing him from a regular weekly schedule. Not only is the actor's appearance protected, but so is his performance. Retakes always can be made if necessary. Furthermore, our technique catches all the spontaneity of live video because the players go through the story in much the same way as they would for a theatre play.

While Fairbanks pioneered the system using 16mm film, a multi-camera set-up using the higher quality 35mm film the system was first used for the game show *You Bet Your Life,* hosted by Groucho Marx.

Isidore Lindenbaum, president of Film Craft Productions, explained in 1952 how the logistics for filming *You Bet Your Life* were worked out.

"[Groucho] needed his audience reaction—their laughs, their applause, even the general feel of audience presence . . . we brought [the audience] before Film Craft's own stage, about 60' by 70', with regular theatre audience seats."

But the presence of a studio audience created more than a few headaches for the sound engineers, who needed to place multiple microphones not only on the stage, but throughout the audience as well. Plus, amplifier speakers were needed for Groucho and the audience to hear each other. The production implemented at least two sound mixers—one on stage, and a second in the audience. The dialogue track recorded separately from the audience track.

As Lindenbaum stressed, "[Groucho] wants the entire program shot in sequence so the audience understands it. He wants no interruptions to cool the audience or his own enthusiasm. He wants no movement of the technical men around the stage, to distract the attention of the audience. He wants no eyes to wander from him. He wants undivided attention. That means film magazines must be loaded and ready for fast changes. That means stand-by cameras must be ready for quick change-over while reloads are made."

The program's director, Robert Dwan, said years later, "We've never taken any particular credit for this, but we really invented the multi-camera system. We wanted to be able to edit and to have Groucho talk to people

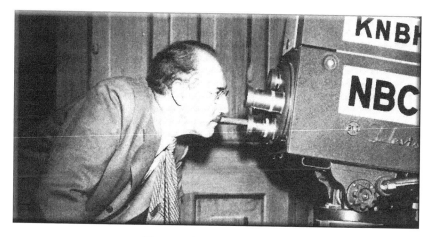

The one, the only…Groucho.

and not have to stop. Videotape wasn't invented at this point. The quality of sixteen-millimeter film wasn't good then, and there was no color television. The obvious thing was to shoot in thirty-five millimeter black and white film. The program used as many as eight 35mm studio cameras for each recording."

"The cameras only carried a ten-minute load of film," Dwan explained. "I decided to use two cameras alongside each other at every position. There were two pointing at Groucho, two for close-ups of contestants, two for a two-shot that could pan from Groucho and the middle contestant to the two contestants, and two cameras that shot all three."

Each cameraman had an assistant at his side plus a man to load all of the cameras. One camera out of each pair would run simultaneously with the others for just under ten minutes, when the second camera of each pair would begin running, while the first cameras were reloaded. "Each pair of cameras would shoot one and half hours in all," Dwan said, "and I could edit with absolute freedom."

Dwan always kept a close-up of Groucho, to keep from missing any remark or facial expression. "I could edit to get at the exact moment when he started his reaction. We started with an elaborate system of lights to establish synchronization. We finally evolved to a simple system where the editor overlapped the film of each pair of cameras."

The Electronicam system, developed by James Caddigan for the DuMont network, used a camera that shot through a conventional orthicon TV camera tube, and sent the beamed image to a 35mm film camera mounted on the side. This technique was used most famously for the "Classic 39" episodes of *The Honeymooners,* produced during the 1955-56 season. The show was shot at the Adelphi Theatre in New York, using three Electronicam units on the stage. Despite the superior picture quality, especially over that of kinescopes, the system died, along with the network itself, later in 1956.

The first use of videotape by the major networks

In the mid-1950s, yet another method of recording television productions revolutionized the medium. Videotape, for use by the major TV studios and networks, was first demonstrated in 1956 by Alexander Poniatoff, founder of the Ampex Corporation.

Before replacing the kinescope system, however, videotape had to be perfected for broadcast quality. Early experiments, conducted by Bing Crosby Enterprises in 1951-52, showed potential, but the image quality was still considered inferior, even to that of kinescopes. Other early versions of videotape were also deemed too limited in their capacity.

Finally, in April 1956, Ampex introduced two-inch video tape, played on a four-head system, first used by CBS on November 30 to record *Douglas Edwards and the News* live in New York. The video was broadcast three hours later for the Pacific Time Zone.

On January 22, 1957, *Truth or Consequences* became the first program to be videotaped for broadcast in all U.S. time zones.

Curiously, it wasn't until 1971 that *All in the Family* became the first sitcom to be videotaped, not filmed, in front of a studio audience.

The first program to be broadcast in color

Even as television's first generation of inventors struggled in the late 1920s and 1930s to produce the first quality pictures and sound with their crude equipment, many observers, and even the engineers themselves, couldn't help but get somewhat ahead of themselves by exploring the idea of color television.

On July 3, 1928, John Logie Baird demonstrated a modified Nipkow scanning disk, on which each of the three spirals of apertures were fitted with lenses of one of the three primary colors. A decade later, on February 4, 1938, Baird sent the world's first color transmission across London.

On August 29, 1940, Dr. Peter C. Goldmark, Chief Television Engineer for CBS, presented a new system of color television. The work had progressed while maintaining a low profile, due to some concerns of upsetting the industry that had been developing only black-and-white television broadcasting. There was some speculation at the time of inner warfare in the industry between those pushing for color TV, and the black-and-white faction that opposed it, because it would mean scrapping millions of dollars' worth of suddenly obsolete equipment.

In 1941 and 1942, color transmissions were broadcast as part of the regular daily schedule from the Chrysler tower to experimental color receivers. Color slides were transmitted for demonstrations, as well as live outdoor scenes, picked up by a color camera from the window of the CBS studios at 15 Vanderbilt Avenue. But progress on these transmissions was affected by the war, requiring television laboratories to yield to military projects such as radar development.

CBS continued to develop an efficient—but far from perfect—color system, but the problem remained that it was not compatible with existing black-and-white TV sets of the time. RCA, parent company of NBC, continued work on its own system—which *was* compatible with black-and-white sets, but in 1950 the FCC deemed the CBS system more desirable, confounding many in the industry. Consequently, adaptors were made available by some TV manufacturers, in order for black-and-white sets to receive the CBS color transmissions. But the majority of TV makers refused to manufacture either the adaptors or the color sets for the CBS system. As RCA continued to improve the picture quality of its color system, the FCC took another look, and in 1953 reversed the earlier decision, adapting the RCA system as the industry standard in the U.S. But since RCA owned the NBC network, the rival networks CBS and ABC dragged their feet to produce color programs that would be using the RCA system.

On August 30, 1953, NBC's fondly-remembered children's show *Kukla, Fran and Ollie* was chosen to introduce the network's recently approved color system. The show was hyped to interest viewers and sponsors, even though there were no color sets in private homes just yet. So, the special nature of the color telecast was lost on all except a handful of network executives and their most valued advertisers.

On New Year's Day 1954, NBC televised the first network *coast-to-coast* color broadcast with its coverage of the Tournament of Roses parade, but the only color sets in use at the time were prototypes set up for public demonstrations.

Since it wouldn't have made sense to broadcast TV programs in color unless there were color TV sets actually available for sale to the public, the next task was to manufacture them. Westinghouse introduced a 15-inch color set and put it on sale in New York on February 28, 1954, with a nearly prohibitive price tag of $1,295. About a month later, on March 25, RCA introduced its own somewhat less expensive 15-inch set, the CT-100, for a price of about $1,000 (still about $6,000 in today's dollars). Programs became available in color only sporadically for a while, as the price of a color set was still way too steep for the average consumer.

The first prime time network series broadcast in color was the live sitcom *The Marriage*, starring the acclaimed husband and wife actors Hume Cronyn and Jessica Tandy. This summer series aired for five weeks in July and August of 1954. A few months later, NBC's *Ford Theatre* became the first weekly filmed color series.

The first color videotaped program, *An Evening with Fred Astaire*, aired on October 17, 1958, and, the following year, NBC first aired *Bonanza* in color. Due to *Bonanza's* established popularity, the series served as an effective catalyst for the network's other weekly dramas to switch to color as well.

However, CBS and ABC remained reluctant to support their competitor NBC's parent company, RCA, which, by 1959, manufactured virtually all color sets in the country. The competition proved so fierce that, in 1960, CBS ceased its color broadcasts for the next *five* years. And ABC didn't air its first color series, *The Jetsons*, until 1962.

These factors, along with the still-high prices of color sets, had color TV traveling down quite a bumpy road on its way to widespread acceptance. By 1962, NBC was airing 2,000 hours of color programming, but, even by 1964, only 3 percent of TV households in the U.S. had a color set.

The next few years proved to be a major turning point for all three networks. By the 1966-67 season, all of the networks' prime time programs were in color, and the prices of color sets continued to come down to more affordable numbers. By 1970, there was at least one TV in 95% of U.S. homes, but color a TV in only 39% of them. It took another few years before the sales of color sets exceeded those of black-and-white TVs.

The first wireless TV remote

Closely following the arrival of the TV dinner in 1954, the next welcome innovation for the TV boom became available when Zenith Electronics introduced the remote control device, enabling viewers to turn the TV on and off, change channels, and adjust the volume without having to leave their easy chairs to do so.

An early version of the TV remote, the Lazy Bones, was developed in 1950, and was connected to the set with a cable. But with the cable came problems involving people tripping as they passed in front of their set.

Eugene Polley devised the "Flash-Matic," a new and improved remote, using photo cells in the set to react to a specialized flashlight, which controlled the various functions depending on which particular light cell it was aimed at. But this also proved to be a faulty design, as the light receivers were easily fooled by sunlight and other lights in the house

Dr. Robert Adler, also with Zenith, suggested an ultrasound method, by which small aluminum rods in the remote would emit a high frequency sound (undetected by humans) to trigger receivers in the TV. Batteries weren't needed. The updated device, called "Space Command," went into production in 1956. It became the industry standard for a quarter-century, until the early 1980s, when infrared technology replaced ultrasound remotes.

Adler worked as engineer for Zenith for sixty years, and, in 1997, he and Polley finally received an Emmy Award for their invention.

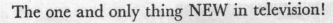

Zenith's "Space Command" remote.

One of the original ideas behind the practice of television "block" programming was for a TV network to provide such a desirable line-up of programs that the viewer would decide against going through the inconvenience of getting up, walking to the TV, and turning the dial to find something on another channel. The arrival of the remote created an even stronger imperative for the broadcast networks to assemble prime time schedules that would dissuade viewers from changing channels, now that they didn't even need to leave their comfy chairs to do so.

For the TV addict in the mid-1950s who could both wolf down a full dinner from an aluminum tray in front of the set, *and* change channels without moving more than a few muscles, life was good indeed.

The first live coast-to-coast TV broadcast

On September 4, 1951, President Harry Truman addressed a conference in San Francisco to formally announce the end of America's post-World War II occupation of Japan. His speech was broadcast live across the U.S., beginning at 7:30 p.m. Pacific time. This was accomplished by having the TV signal bounce along a network of radio receivers installed by AT&T, and sending it across the Colorado Rockies to facilities in Omaha, Nebraska (the furthest reach of New York-based network TV at the time). From there, the signal was carried eastward by the recently-completed coaxial cable system, thus enabling the transmission to travel fully coast-to-coast. Ninety-four of the country's 107 TV stations carried the broadcast, reaching 95% of households owning televisions (almost thirteen million families). The live picture, as seen in New York, was reported by *The New York Times* as having "excellent clarity and compared favorably with the programs of local origin. The contrast was of first-rate quality and there was no distortion."

The success of the broadcast created great excitement in the television industry, and, later than autumn, on November 18, the premiere installment of Edward R. Murrow's *See It Now* program treated viewers to the first live coast-to-coast commercial TV broadcast. To illustrate the capabilities of the new video technology, Murrow and director Don Hewitt (future creator and producer of *60 Minutes*) presented two side-by side monitors on the wall of the control booth—one monitor carried a live shot of the Statue of Liberty in New York harbor, and the other a live shot of the San Francisco Bay Bridge. In his excitement, and perhaps to show off just a bit, Murrow asked the cameramen on each coast to adjust their shots slightly, and each complied. Such a trick goes unnoticed today, as news anchors in their studios often ask reporters and their cameramen to "go wide" or pan across the newsworthy scene in question, but on that November 18, 1951, even the usually stone-faced Murrow could barely contain his giddiness.

The first broadcast transmitted via satellite

Each time we see a TV news reporter speaking to us live from another part of the world, with a clear, instantaneous picture and crisp sound, we rarely if ever bother to consider the technology that brings the report to us, allowing us to witness, and almost feel an event as it happens, even half a world away. This is all thanks to several generations of satellites that can be traced back to the original Telstar.

On July 10, 1962, the Telstar communication satellite, built by Bell labs and launched by NASA, achieved orbit 3,000 miles above the Earth. The 350-pound device had to wait until its sixth orbit over the Atlantic to achieve line-of-sight range with an AT&T tracking antenna in Andover, Maine, which sent an image of an American flag (with the dome-shaped antenna in the background) up to the satellite. Telstar then bounced the image to an antenna in Holmdel, New Jersey, for broadcast across the country. Strains of "America the Beautiful" and "The Star Spangled Banner" accompanied the image.

On the following orbit, a new image was transmitted to receiving antennas in England and France, thus achieving history's first intercontinental live television feed via satellite. The first images viewers in those countries saw were those of Vice President Johnson and other officials as they witnessed the event from Washington, D.C.

Also on the seventh orbit, the first two-way phone conversation via

New "TELSTAR" relays phone calls and TV pictures for first time!

Bell System microwave-in-sky satellite is latest communications triumph for America arising from telephone research

The world's first private enterprise communications satellite is now being used for dramatic experiments in relaying telephone calls and television internationally.

Its name: Telstar. It was launched from Cape Canaveral at Bell System expense by the National Aeronautics and Space Administration.

Telstar receives signals beamed to it from a ground station, amplifies them and transmits them to another station on the ground below—perhaps an ocean away from the first one. The new satellite thus acts as a microwave relay station in the sky, enabling voices, TV pictures and data messages to leap thousands of miles in a new and exciting way.

The ground stations in the U.S. now being used for Telstar were built by the Bell System at Andover, Maine, and Holmdel, New Jersey. Organizations abroad have built stations in England and France. The latter, a near replica of the station in Maine, was assembled with Bell System cooperation. A receiving station in Italy will be ready late this year, and another in West Germany next year.

Telstar is a major experimental step toward a world-wide satellite communications system that was first proposed as a practical venture at Bell Telephone Laboratories. Progress toward such a system has depended on many contributions by the private communications industry, including six basic components—the transistor, the solar battery, the traveling wave tube, ruby masers, the waveguide, and new antennas for the ground stations with innovations in circuitry—direct outgrowths of Bell System research and development.

Above all else, Telstar is the latest achievement in an unending Bell System quest—the search for ways to make your telephone service still better, more economical, and more useful.

BELL TELEPHONE SYSTEM

INSIDE GROUND STATION "RADOME" AT ANDOVER, MAINE. Giant antenna (note man near rim of horn) concentrates signals to Telstar in a narrow, powerful beam. The same antenna also receives extremely weak signals coming from Telstar and amplifies them billions of times.

Telstar.

satellite took place between Johnson and Frederick R. Kappel, chairman of the board of AT&T. Although it was a "domestic" call, Telstar had also ushered in the era of direct, transatlantic and trans-global phone calls.

The event was hailed as the greatest advance in communications since

Morse's telegraph. In fact, all three major TV networks interrupted their regular programming to televise the successful experiment live. The next day, newspapers such as the *New York Times* devoted front page headlines to Telstar's achievement.

The first live TV transmission from space

The first attempt by the American space program to transmit live TV pictures from a manned spacecraft to Earth came during the last Mercury flight, Faith 7, in May of 1963. Astronaut Gordon Cooper handled a ten-pound camera to transmit images of himself in the capsule as well as views of Earth through the window. However, there was limited light in the capsule, and the camera only provided single images taken every two seconds—resulting in what was more of a quick series of stills, rather than what we would refer to today as a "live stream" TV signal. The following year, during the flight of the Soviet spacecraft Voskhod I in 1964, the Russian cosmonauts reportedly sent TV pictures of themselves back to Earth.

But the major breakthrough in space-to-Earth television came during the Apollo 7 mission in October 1968. Apollo 7 was the first manned mission since the tragic Apollo 1 launch pad fire on January 27, 1967, in which all three astronauts were killed (Apollo missions 2 through 6 were unmanned tests). The Apollo 7 crew of Donn Eisele, Walter Cunningham, and commander Walter Schirra, orbited the Earth for 11 days, during which time the astronauts greeted Earthbound viewers with the first live television transmission.

Despite the historic significance of sending the first live TV pictures from space, the crew, especially Schirra, didn't give the task a very high priority on their to-do list. In fact, they preferred not to have it on the list at all. The astronauts had been in conflict with NASA for several weeks prior to the flight regarding the use of a TV camera, calling it a "stunt" dreamed up by NASA as a public relations gimmick. Moreover, Schirra's foul mood on the day of the proposed telecast (the second day of the mission) was prompted by his bad head cold, hunger, and problems with the spacecraft's waste water dumping system. The crew also needed to make preparations for the delicate task of achieving a rendezvous with the shell of a booster rocket in orbit, to simulate a rescue mission.

The live telecast from the command module was to take place at 11:00 a.m. Eastern time, but Schirra refused to deal with it, citing the need to concentrate on the timing of the rendezvous. The mission controllers insisted he proceed with the TV transmission. Schirra would have none of it. "You have added two burns to this flight schedule," he scolded the flight controllers on the ground. "You have added a urine water dump and we have a new vehicle up here and I tell you this flight TV will be delayed without further discussion until after the rendezvous." He canceled the planned demonstration of the four-pound TV camera, leaving the controllers at the Manned Spacecraft Center in Houston literally speechless for a long moment. However, once the rendezvous was completed, Schirra then agreed to the TV broadcast for the following day.

The Apollo 7 astronauts greet television viewers from orbit.

The next morning, the Apollo crew, in a cheerier mood, did take out the camera and hosted a seven-minute live broadcast from 150 miles above the Earth, showing viewers the inside of the capsule and pointing the camera out a window to catch the site of the Southern U.S. below them.

The first home video recorder

When videotape became a means for network television productions to record, edit and preserve studio-based programs in the mid-1950s, the technology was not considered something destined to be of use in the average home.

A decade later, in June 1965, Sony introduced an early but primitive commercial home video recorder set, one that used reel-to-reel tapes, like an audio tape recorder, within a large console unit. But its price tag of $995.00 was an astronomical figure in 1965. It was clear that a multitude of improvements needed to be made.

By 1972, Sony had made progress, and introduced the U-Matic VCR, which used ¾" tape cartridges in a player-recorder, touted in its advertising copy as "a revolutionary new means of communication." The ad then offered a lengthy explanation of the basic concept of a videotape system, its capabilities, and possibilities for commercial—and especially medical—use. The ad also mused that, "perhaps, someday, there'll be a U-matic in every living room."

This larger, ¾" tape format did indeed find widespread use over the next two decades, in broadcasting, business promotional productions, and other commercial needs. But the unwieldy size of the tape cartridges and player/recorders were still not convenient for home use.

In the spring of 1975, Sony made its true breakthrough, with the introduction of the Betamax videocassette recorder, although the manufacturer initially produced it only as part of a larger console that also housed a built-in TV monitor. Less than a year later, however, the more desirable stand-alone Betamax recorder hit the market, greatly spiking sales. As the introductory ad explained, the Betamax "can actually videotape something off one channel while you're watching another channel" to be easily played back at a later time. Not only that, the machine's timer "can be set to automatically

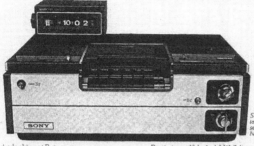

The first ad for Sony's Betamax.

videotape that program while you're not there." This concept seems ho-hum in the age of digital video recorders, but it was almost too good to believe for avid television viewers—and just about everyone else—at the time.

That same year, Sony competitor JVC introduced the VHS format, whose tape cartridges were bigger than Betamax tapes, but also ran twice as long—two hours to Beta's one-hour. Some observers detected the slightest loss of picture sharpness compared to that of Beta, but a fierce competition for the public's favor ended when VHS overtook Beta as the format of choice by the majority of American users.

Still other home video formats competed for the market place in those early days. Quasar introduced the VR-1000 "Great Time Machine" that used tapes even bigger than VHS tapes, but could still record only two hours at a time. In addition, the machine was quite heavy and bulky. It remained on the market for less than a year.

In comedian Jay Leno's book, *Leading with My Chin,* he relates the story (with a dose of hyperbole) of how he rushed to buy a VCR in time to record his first TV appearance in 1977:

> I paid twelve hundred dollars for a basic machine...completely incompatible with anything available now, it seemed to be steam-driven and made of cast iron. It weighed three hundred pounds and—as best I could tell—was bulletproof. The most you could tape was a half-hour at a time. And the tapes were huge, the size of a human head. You'd load them in and hear *caaaa-chonnnnnnk!* Then you'd press play and the lights would dim in the house. The belts on it would propel a Harley. Just a monstrosity. But, at least, I was now ready to record myself for posterity.

A decade later, in July 1987, fully half of the households in the U.S. included a VCR, and the number increased to over 75% by the mid-1990s. The machines became nearly as common as televisions themselves, until DVRs began to encroach on that market.

The first HDTV is introduced

"Japan flipped a switch this morning," announced *The New York Times* on November 25, 1991, "and started a new era in broadcasting history: Eight hours a day of high-definition television."

The startlingly sharp HDTV images on the screens of public demonstration sets came courtesy of a new satellite serving Japan, making that country's Hi-Vision system the first in the world. By doing so, Japan beat out the similar efforts in the U.S. and Europe to create a standard high definition TV system.

It was no coincidence that HDTV was unveiled on November 25, which numerically reads 11/25. There are 1,125 lines composing the high definition screen.

However, the Japanese system used analog-based technology, at a time when a more cutting edge, digital system—one that would be compatible with computer use and data storage—lay in the sights of U.S. video engineers. Another drawback to Japan's new system was the initial price. An HDTV set cost a whopping $30,000 (yes, you read that right—thirty thousand dollars).

CHAPTER 4
FIRSTS IN TELEVISION
NEWS COVERAGE

The first major news events to be covered by television

When New York governor Al Smith accepted his Democratic presidential nomination in 1928, he delivered his acceptance speech in Albany, rather than at the convention's venue in Dallas (before 1932, nominees did not attend their parties' national conventions, until Franklin Roosevelt appeared in person at the Democratic national convention to accept his nomination). Smith's acceptance speech in Albany was televised by WYG in Schenectady, using an early version of a compact, mobile camera engineered by Alexanderson, making the transmission the first remote TV news report in history.

A few years later, on March 3, 1932, the first case of television reporting a crime story occurred in connection with the kidnapping of Lindbergh baby, the son of legendary aviator Charles Lindbergh and his wife, Anne.

At CBS station W2XAB in New York, a photo of the baby was broadcast continuously from 2 to 6 p.m. that day, and at fifteen-minute intervals in the evening. Station director William Schudt, claimed that the signal carrying the image had a 1,000-mile radius, and was received by several thousand TV sets in the area. Newspapers reported that "a number of phone calls were received at the station from observers in the New York district who picked up the baby's image, which they said compared favorably with a newspaper half-tone picture."

On March 10, 1933, experimental Los Angeles TV station, W6XAO, owned by television pioneer Don Lee, began semi-regular broadcasting over a thirty mile radius. On that same day, an earthquake hit the city, prompting Lee to send a newsreel film crew to shoot footage of the damage. The film was processed and televised by the next day, to be seen mostly on demonstration televisions in the windows of department and appliance stores.

About three months later, on June 23 in New York, an even more shocking incident was caught on camera, but was not broadcast to any receiving sets among the public. NBC cameraman Ross Plaisted, taking part in experimental work atop a mobile camera truck parked in Rockefeller Center caught the sight of a woman plunging to her death from the Time Life building across the plaza. Plaisted had been taking routine shots of the plaza for a series of tests, and happened to swing his camera around to the falling woman just as she was about to hit the ground. The image was visible only on monitors in the control room for the engineers to see. It was later reported that the woman, twenty-eight-year-old Marion Perloff, was an employee of the Girl Scouts Inc. headquarters, and had been, just minutes earlier, waving to her co-workers below as they left for a bus trip and picnic for the day. She considered joining them, but when she couldn't reach her sister by phone to inform her she'd be late getting home, she decided not to go with her colleagues. Minutes after the bus left, Perloff plunged from a window overlooking West 49th Street—the first death of a person ever caught live by a television camera.

In November of that year, a fire broke out on Ward's Island in New York, while an NBC mobile unit happened to be setting up shots at the Astoria outdoor swimming pool just across the river. The camera caught the fire scene and transmitted it live to sets in the area, and those who saw the telecast described the pictures as "amazingly clear."

The first news bulletin on TV

On December 7, 1941, the "date which will live in infamy," Japan attacked the Pearl Harbor naval base in Hawaii, and several other Pacific islands, a few minutes before 8:00 a.m. local time, 2:00 p.m. Eastern time.

In New York, local radio station WOR and radio network affiliates of CBS and NBC all interrupted their broadcasts with the bulletin off the wire services; they all did so between 2:26 and 2:30 p.m.

It's been estimated that there were still fewer than 10,000 TV sets in the entire country at the time, and half of those were in New York, where only two commercial TV stations were operating, WNBT (NBC) and WCBW (CBS). This was only five months after the FCC issued the first commercial licenses for television. DuMont's station W2XWV was still experimental, and not yet licensed.

On December 7, only WNBT was on the air, as WCBW did not broadcast on Sundays. When the WNBT newsroom teletypes first received the bulletins of the Pearl Harbor attack, the station had just begun running the film *Millionaire Playboy*, starring radio comedian Joe Penner. Shortly after 3:30 p.m., station announcer Ray Forrest interrupted the film with the news. Sam Cuff, host of the station's *Face of the War* program, had at his disposal a number of maps to help illustrate the nature and location of the attack. One studio camera was pointed at the Associated Press teletype to capture the moment of each new bulletin's arrival. Cuff was eventually joined by his *Face of the War* colleagues to analyze the incoming information.

Meanwhile, with WCBW off the air, that station's news writer Robert Skedgell, news reader Richard Hubbell, and program director Gilbert Seldes heard the news and scrambled to get from their homes to the station and unlock its doors. Skedgell and Hubbell had been collaborators on the station's 15-minute weekday news broadcasts, and by 3:30 p.m., WCBW was on the air with the first reports, right on the heels of WNBT. Like their competitor, they had to rely on maps of the Pacific and sporadic updates throughout the day, but stayed on the air long into the evening (there are differing versions of how long the marathon broadcast lasted—most accounts concur it was at least nine hours). Hubbell was joined by Major General Fielding Eliot and Fletcher Pratt. Linton Wells provided breaking news.

The next day, when President Roosevelt addressed Congress to ask for a formal declaration of war, newsreel cameras were present, but no arrangement had been made to bring a television camera to the House chamber for a live video feed. Instead, a shot of an American flag waving in the breeze was used on TV to accompany the audio portion of the speech.

In the years following the end of World War II, the Cold War between the U.S. and U.S.S.R. continued to get colder as it entered the 1950s. Thus, in December 1951, President Truman created a system for delivering news bulletins of special urgency. The CONELRAD public alert system was designed to warn the public, via reports on designated radio frequencies, of an impending attack, presumably via Soviet bombers carrying nuclear weapons (CONELRAD was an abbreviation of the rather ominous sounding "Control of Electromagnetic Radiation").

When intercontinental ballistic missiles later replaced slower-moving bomber planes as the more likely means to deliver nuclear warheads, CONELRAD needed to be either updated or replaced. On August 5, 1963, the system was officially discontinued and replaced by the Emergency Broadcast System. The EBS's purpose was basically the same as that of CONELRAD—to give the public as early and accurate a warning of an imminent emergency as quickly as possible, whether it be an attack by a foreign country, or a regional crisis, such as a natural disaster.

The EBS was never used for a nationwide alert, but regional broadcast interruptions, mostly for natural disasters such as tornadoes and severe hurricanes, were used thousands of times during its years in use. In 1997, the EBS was replaced by the Emergency Alert System.

The first network-produced television news program

Before newscasts as we know them today were developed for TV, the medium relied almost exclusively on theatrical newsreel films, already edited and narrated, to bring the world's events to the picture tube.

Even before television's "official" opening day on April 30, 1939, the *March of Time* newsreel series proved the most popular among NBC's experimental transmissions. Arrangements were made with the film series' producers to use back releases of the feature. *Broadcasting* magazine reported that NBC favored the series because "the film has the continuity desired in television, and the *March of Time* ordinarily has many of the close-ups and intermediate shots that televise best over an all-electronic system."

During World War II, brief news broadcasts produced with small budgets began to appear more often. The programs of this time were anchored by known and respected radio reporters, who sat behind desks with little or no visual aids as they read headlines to the camera. NBC's *The War as it Happens*, as the title suggests, basically ran newsreel footage of developments pertaining to the war, with no regular field correspondents or news directors. It began airing in New York in April 1944, but it was later fed to the Philadelphia and Schenectady affiliates, making it the first newscast seen on a network. The *CBS Television News* also appeared in 1944, airing for fifteen minutes on the nights of the week the network was on the air.

The NBC Television Newsreel first aired on August 8, 1945, right in between the dropping of the atomic bombs on Hiroshima and Nagasaki. When Japan surrendered a few days later, the program included shots of the jubilant crowds in Times Square.

The first network evening news anchorman

General Electric's Schenectady station W2XB (a.k.a. WGY and WRGB) has rightful claim to many television "firsts," so it stands to reason that much of its early, primitive programming content, transmitted from its simple studio to the handful of TV sets in the area, could be considered the first of *anything*. Strictly speaking then, the station's Kolin Hager, already experienced in radio drama, became the first American TV newscaster on May 10, 1928, when he first offered farm and weather reports on Tuesday, Thursday, and Friday afternoons.

John Cameron Swayze began a daily TV newscast on KMBC in Kansas City in the 1930s (some sources say 1933, others say 1937). The program did not last long, and Swayze once recalled only that it was "kind of fun because it was novel."

The first nightly news program, DuMont's *News from Washington*, premiered on June 16, 1947, with Walter Compton as anchor. The show ran for just under a year.

The man generally recognized as the first true network anchorman of a nightly newscast is Douglas Edwards, who, on August 15, 1948, launched the era of network television news programming with the debut of the 15-minute *Douglas Edwards with the News* on CBS. He kept the job for fourteen years, until 1962, when Walter Cronkite stepped in to begin his own legendary tenure on the air.

The first network evening news anchorwoman

In 1948, ABC hired veteran print and radio journalist Pauline Frederick as the first newswoman to work full time for a major TV network.

Frederick's early experience included writing fluff pieces for several local papers in the Harrisburg, Pennsylvania, area. After attending American University in Washington, D.C., she first managed to make a name for herself in the male-dominated radio news profession by conducting interviews not with various world leaders and ambassadors, but with their wives. This allowed her the opportunity to cover world events from a perspective none of her male counterparts had attempted, or even considered. She returned to print journalism in the 1930s until she was hired by ABC radio in 1938.

The next decade offered its share of steps both forward and backward for Frederick's career. During her first year on ABC television in 1948, she hosted her own weekday news program, *Pauline Frederick Reports*, making her the first female host of a regularly scheduled news program. But it was a daytime show, rather than airing in a more coveted early evening slot. In 1953, NBC News hired her as its United Nations correspondent, giving her far greater exposure and making her a household name for the next two decades, during which time she set many precedents for female broadcast journalists to emulate.

Even with Frederick's breakthroughs, it was still slow-going for women broadcast journalists seeking high profile positions on the networks, especially in prime time slots. It wasn't until December 12, 1976, that NBC

Barbara Walters made waves in TV news in 1976.

correspondent Cassie Mackin began her year-long stint as the regular Sunday anchor for the *NBC Nightly News,* making her the first woman to serve as sole host of a network evening news program. Her position was made possible in part by the departure of Barbara Walters for ABC.

This happened when, in an effort to help boost ratings, ABC lured Walters from her long-running stint as co-host of NBC's *Today* show, with an offer of one million dollars per year to co-host the *ABC Evening News* with Harry Reasoner. Walters had specialized in celebrity interviews to that point, creating the perception that she was more interested in mingling with glamorous Hollywood types and reporting gossip than in doing hard journalism. Her new colleagues in the world of evening news broadcasting did not take kindly to her much-hyped promotion. Their remarks at the time would be considered blatantly sexist today (of course, they were blatantly sexist in 1976 as well).

For example, upon the announcement of Walters's promotion, CBS veteran news anchor Walter Cronkite bemoaned the idea that "all of our efforts to hold network television news aloof from show business had failed." David Brinkley felt compelled to remind us that "being an anchor is not just a matter of sitting in front of a camera and looking pretty." And Walters's new co-anchor Reasoner was so upset with the prospect of sharing his on-air news desk with her that ABC briefly considered scrapping the notion altogether. But, while Reasoner reneged and swallowed mighty hard to get through each newscast with Walters at his side, the tension between them proved too distracting. Roone Arledge later recalled, "On his own, Harry was excellent . . . clearly a star at ABC. On her own, Barbara was fabulous—so long as she wasn't anchoring. But put the two of them together and what you had was like arriving for a dinner party at the house of a couple trying to maintain a truce in front of the world while waiting to claw each other's eyes out."

In 1978, the partnership was disbanded, as ABC totally revamped its evening newscast—without either Reasoner or Walters—under a new name, *World News Tonight,* and a curious new format, dividing the anchor duties between Frank Reynolds in Washington, Max Robinson in Chicago, and Peter Jennings in London. Meanwhile, Walters found a new home as co-host of the ABC news/magazine program *20/20,* as well as host of occasional, highly-rated celebrity interview specials.

On June 1, 1993, CBS attempted teaming *CBS Evening News* anchor Dan Rather with Connie Chung. The results, like those of the Reasoner-Walters fiasco, were disappointing, and for similar reasons. Rather had been the sole anchor of the newscast since Walter Cronkite's retirement in 1981, and did not relish sharing his on-air duties with Chung, whose own relative lack of hard news reporting did not bode well for their partnership. Chung left her weeknight co-anchor position in 1995.

On September 5, 2006, Rather retired as anchor, and was replaced by Katie Couric, making her the first female *solo* anchor of a network weeknight news program. And, in December 2009, Diane Sawyer began her run as the sole female anchor of ABC's *World News Tonight*.

Couric's tenure concluded in May 2011, and Sawyer left *World News Tonight* in September 2014.

The first all-news cable network

In January 1970, Comsat executive Dan Karasik predicted that, at some point in the coming decade, ". . . I can't think of an event of any importance that won't be on television world-wide. We'll see a world broadcasting union with operating centers going twenty-four hours a day, planning and sharing programs . . . Maybe we'll see a daily or twice-daily world-news round-up, with live reports from many parts of the globe—wherever news is happening. The world will be one big mixing pot. And culturally, we'll all be much richer people because of it."

Karasik's prediction proved to be remarkably accurate. Later that same year, a successful and flamboyant business tycoon named Ted Turner—president of an Atlanta area billboard company—purchased WRJR-TV, a small UHF station in the city. A decade later, on June 1, 1980, Turner launched his Cable News Network.

The formative years of cable TV saw a number of broadcasting concepts and networks succeed, fail, or evolve. Even so, the idea of a 24-hour, all-news network struck many industry leaders and observers as ludicrous. But the ever confident Turner took the skepticism and mockery in stride. "I knew it was gonna be a hit before it went on the air," he once told longtime CNN talk show host Larry King.

CNN becomes the world's first all-news cable network.

On June 1, CNN news anchors David Walker and Lois Hart welcomed viewers to a new era of news broadcasting, with the bustle of the open newsroom in full view behind them. Other on-air personalities helping to launch the network included Lou Waters and Kathleen Sullivan. But construction of the newsroom hadn't yet been completed by that first day, and the sounds of drills and hammers punctuated some of the early programs. The many on-air technical glitches were due in part to equipment that hadn't even been tested before their installation.

Atlanta served as the network headquarters, with major bureaus in Washington, D.C. and New York City. Respected ABC veteran Bernard Shaw took on the role of Washington bureau chief, and NBC anchor Mary Alice Williams left that network to head the New York bureau, located just off the lobby of one of the World Trade Center towers (complete with a glass wall enabling passers-by on the concourse to peek in on the newsroom activity). The first foreign news bureaus were set up in London, Rome, and Peking.

In those early days of the network's operation, it became apparent that a bigger staff would be needed, but the limited hiring budget couldn't allow for it. The solution was to recruit college broadcasting majors from around the country, offer them a brief introductory seminar on how to use the CNN studio equipment, and have them learn the rest on the job. Little pay and long hours were the order of the day for all CNN employees, but the certainty that they were a part of a revolutionary undertaking provided an energy and loyalty all its own. So began CNN's history of covering major events and breaking news from around the world and reporting them live, often beating the long-established major broadcast networks to the punch.

Skepticism about CNN's chances of success endured well into its first year. In the September 1980 issue of *Panorama* magazine, broadcast journalism expert Edwin Diamond reported his early impressions of the network's first few months of on-air operations. "CNN is not very good journalistically," he said. "Can anyone, even with unlimited resources offer intelligent, useful, ultimately clarifying news and information around the clock?"

But the network had its supporters, including the head of ABC News,

Roone Arledge. "Any 24-hour news service can work, should work," he said, in that same issue of *Panorama*. "I was very impressed with their operation when they first started. It is serious; it is interesting. I'm a little troubled that, having all that time, they don't use it for more important functions. I don't know whether Turner will survive or not. My gut feeling is that he's under-financed, but maybe not."

About eighteen months after CNN's launch, on January 1, 1982, a sister network, CNN-2, began broadcasting. Renamed CNN Headline News the following year, its broadcasts were designed more as packaged half-hours, rather than as a continuous stream of news that had defined its older sibling.

CNN enjoyed sixteen years as the only 24-hour news network, making it television's version of the *New York Times*'s status as America's "newspaper of record." By late 1987, the network had reached more than half of all U.S. television homes. But on July 15, 1996, MSNBC (created as a partnership between NBC and Microsoft), began its own 24-hour news operation, and, just three months later, on October 7, the Fox News Channel kicked off its inaugural broadcast.

Competition among the three cable news networks grew in intensity in the years since, causing gains and losses of viewership by all three at various times. While Fox News and its more politically conservative philosophies were counter-balanced by the liberal leaning MSNBC, CNN more or less held the center (and felt the inevitable criticism from both sides at times). But CNN has also seen an erosion of viewership of its daily afternoon and prime time programs, boosted only by coverage of major breaking news stories.

CHAPTER 5
FIRSTS IN COVERAGE
OF POLITICAL EVENTS

The first president to appear on television

President Franklin D. Roosevelt was known for his command of radio, both in formal speeches and in his "fireside chats" to comfort Americans throughout the Depression. He also has a place in television history as having been the first president in office to appear on television. As described earlier, his speech declaring the World's Fair in New York open on April 30, 1939, was telecast by NBC.

Strictly speaking, this was not Roosevelt's first appearance on a TV screen. In September 1936, an experimental transmission in New York—sent from the new antenna atop the Empire State Building, and received on just a handful of television receivers in the area—included newsreel film footage of presidential candidates Roosevelt and New York's governor, Alf Landon. Roosevelt's footage was shot as he spoke from a train observation platform, while Landon was seen giving a speech at an unidentified locale. The transmission of this newsreel footage was reported to have been received clearly on Long Island, and was presumed to have had similarly sharp pictures and sound reaching substantial sections of New Jersey and Connecticut as well.

When Roosevelt died in April of 1945, he was the first president whose death was covered on television, as stations across the country paid tribute. *Televiser* magazine reported that "all commercial telecasts were cancelled for a three-day period and stations devoted programs to various phases of the late Chief Executive's life."

The first political convention to be televised

The first telecast of a national political convention took place with the opening of the 1940 Republican National Convention at Convention Hall in Philadelphia. The broadcast was relayed to New York's NBC station W2XBS via a 108-mile wire circuit (most of which was a coaxial cable) developed by Bell Telephone.

The telecast opened outside the hall with pick-ups of the crowd and shots of the arriving delegates. Viewers then saw Chairman John D.M. Hamilton calling the convention to order, and former presidential candidate Alfred M. Landon posing for photographers with the Kansas delegation's banner.

In Philadelphia, television came in handy to accommodate the overflow of spectators who could not get into Convention Hall. As many as sixty monitors were reportedly put in place in South Museum, adjacent to the convention venue.

NBC claimed a total of 50,000 viewers (not 50,000 TV *sets*) of the proceedings among the Philadelphia, New York, and Schenectady affiliates. According to an NBC spokesman, most of the TV sets in New York were in bars, hotels, and department stores such as Bloomingdales, where an estimated crowd of one hundred gathered to watch. At Gimbels, about seventy-five people assembled to look in on the convention coverage. In addition, an estimated 1,000 visitors to the RCA exhibit at the World's Fair viewed the telecast in fifteen-minute shifts.

After all was said and done, the Republicans nominated Wendell Willkie to run against Roosevelt—with F.D.R.'s famous landslide re-election to follow.

The first political campaign telecast

On October 11, 1932, the first political campaign program of any kind aired on W2XAB (CBS) in New York. The program was presented by the stage and screen division of the Democratic National Committee.

Among those who appeared on the half-hour program were Helen Morgan, then starring in *Show Boat* on Broadway; Toni Canzoneri, lightweight boxing champion; Rosamond Pinchot, niece of Governor Pinchot of Pennsylvania; Melvina Passmore, who sang at the Democratic National Convention in Chicago the previous June, and Wayne Pierson, who acted as host.

Newspaper men and engineers watched the show in the Chrysler Building as it was picked up by the Myers Electrical Research Laboratory.

As *The New York Times* reported, "The images that appeared on the screen, two feet square, in the semi-dark laboratory room were quite clear, and the performers were readily recognizable. Onlookers were reminded of the earliest motion pictures."

The first televised presidential debate

The first and perhaps still the most well-known televised debate between presidential candidates took place between Democratic Senator John F. Kennedy and Republican Vice-President Richard Nixon on September 26, 1960. Held in Chicago and broadcast on CBS, this first of four debates between Kennedy and Nixon became a transformative moment in the history of American politics, television, and the merging of the two.

The actual content of the candidates' statements was not nearly as noteworthy as the aesthetics of the TV broadcast itself. Firstly, Kennedy chose to wear a dark suit for the event, which contrasted well against the studio background. But Nixon's grey suit caused him to blend into the set behind him. And, while both candidates declined make-up beforehand, Kennedy had his applied privately, by his own staff. Nixon did so as well, in secret, but his five o'clock shadow couldn't be obscured. On camera, he also had a tendency to perspire and flutter his eyes nervously, which was often caught by reaction shots as Kennedy spoke. The overall effect was one that showed Kennedy as more appealing to the eye, although listeners of the debate on radio gave Nixon the edge.

The presence of television at political events began to influence the events themselves, long before the Kennedy-Nixon debate. As early as 1948, during the Democratic and Republican national conventions, speakers first realized they needed to be conscious of the TV audience, and address not only the delegates on the convention floor, but the viewers at home as well. In a photo story featuring shots of various prominent statesmen being prepared with make-up before their respective televised speeches, *Life* magazine noted, "Television not only covered but influenced the convention: for one thing, it made men who would once have shuddered at the idea submit to greasepaint. In the future it will probably change the whole shape of political conventions into a more dramatic and faster moving show."

Despite this growing influence of television in politics, Richard Nixon's unfortunate appearance during that first debate in 1960, and his narrow loss to Kennedy in November, no doubt had much to do with the decision to forego the practice during his successful run for president in 1968, and for his re-election campaign in 1972.

Televised debates returned in 1976, with Jimmy Carter challenging incumbent Gerald Ford. Each presidential campaign since then has included a series of televised debates among the lead and vice-presidential candidates.

The first presidential election night to be televised

Election night reporting on television has come to mean the virtually instantaneous flow of information, voting returns, and statistics reported from all over the country, accompanied by swirling graphics and special effects, live remotes, brightly-lit studios, and state-of-the-art anchor desks and consoles.

It's been a long journey from the first-ever national election night report on television, transmitted in New York by W2XAB on November 8, 1932. Beginning at 8:00 p.m., placards with the latest returns, and photos of the principle candidates, were held in front of the station's TV camera. While awaiting updated results, viewers were treated to what was described at the time as "a group of studio entertainers."

How times have changed.

The first televised State-of-the-Union speech

Harry Truman was the first president to reap the advantages of television's post-war era, and was himself involved in a number of television firsts. He made his own first network television appearance at a Navy Day celebration in New York in 1945, carried by NBC to its Schenectady and Philadelphia affiliates. The event was held in Central Park, and special arrangements were made for recovering sailors and marines to see the broadcast on TV in a number of New York hospitals.

Truman's State of the Union speech to Congress on January 6, 1947, was the first to be televised. Later that same year, on October 5, he also delivered the first TV address from the White House.

Truman was also the first president to add a television set to the White House accoutrements. He had an RCA television installed in the Oval Office in January 1947, to view the first TV coverage of the House of Representatives' new session. Later in the year, Truman reportedly used the set to catch part of the World Series.

In addition, after he won the 1948 presidential election, Truman's inauguration was the first presidential inauguration to be televised. An estimated ten million people—more people than had seen the thirty-one previous inaugurations combined—watched him take the oath of office on January 20, 1949.

Four years later, on January 20, 1953, President Eisenhower's inauguration was the first to be telecast coast-to-coast.

The first live Presidential press conference

The first Presidential press conferences to be televised were not broadcast live, but were filmed and edited before airtime. The first press conference to air on TV was held by President Eisenhower on the morning of January 19, 1955, at the State Department. It lasted just over a half-hour, but was subject to some editing—and White House approval—before a 28-minute version aired later that evening.

President Kennedy became the first president to hold a live press conference on January 25, 1961, just days after his inauguration. It was covered by all three networks and, like Eisenhower's, was held at the State Department. Kennedy's lasted closer to thirty-eight minutes, during which he answered thirty-one questions.

CHAPTER 6
FIRSTS IN SPORTS COVERAGE

The first sports event to be televised

In 1931, it was reported that a baseball game in Japan had been televised there, the only evidence being a photograph found in a Japanese magazine. The photo was reproduced via an artist's rendering for an issue of *Television News* magazine in the U.S. The accompanying article could only surmise by the drawing that, "judging by the original photograph…the televisor utilized for picking up the baseball game was a stationary affair, and it evidently was focused across the home plate." There were actually two televised games played in Tokyo that year. The first took place between two college teams on February 17 at Tazuka Baseball Ground, and was televised via closed circuit to the Electrical Laboratory at Waseda University. The second game, played on September 27 by two public school teams at the Tazuka field, was for over-the-air public viewing, although there were only a handful of privately-owned TV sets in Tokyo at the time.

At the same time, CBS studio W2XAB in New York conducted a series of experimental transmissions of boxing matches in the studio; these were not sanctioned events.

If you want to include sports involving four-legged athletes, the running of the English Derby at the Epsom race track in England was successfully transmitted on June 1, 1932, to an audience of 2,500 watching a large projected image in the Metropole Cinema in London, fifteen miles away. It was John Logie Baird's latest in a long line of successful demonstrations to make television a viable tool of mass communication and entertainment.

Two weeks before the race, Baird and his team set up a telephone cable system for both audio and visual signals. Inside their van, a large round drum, affixed with thirty rectangular mirrors, was set to rotate at 750 rpm, like a large, modified Nipkow disk. "When revolving, therefore," explained *Television News*, "a succession of images of the scene reflected on the mirrors was thrown on to a lens, and these were made to move over three distinct apertures admitting the different degrees of light and shade comprising the scene, to three individual photo-electric cells . . . " Amplifiers increased the signal strength before sending it to the Baird Company's control room at Long Acre, London. From there, they were relayed to the back of the stage at the Metropole Cinema, where the television receiving equipment had been installed (including a mirrored drum identical to that in the van at the track). "Careful matching, framing and phasing, these three zones of thirty light strips built themselves into a composite picture, the resultant size being ten feet wide and eight feet high. It was sufficiently brilliant to be seen clearly in any part of the house, and the special nature of the translucent screen enabled the images to be seen from any angle of view."

The excitement within the theater perhaps exceeded that at the racetrack itself. With amplifier speakers set on the stage, the audience first heard from a commentator reporting from the scene. As an eyewitness account described, "The curtains [on the stage] were not drawn aside until the commentator announced that the horses were approaching the range of the Epsom daylight transmitter. When they did, a murmur of amazement spread over the whole house, and as it dawned on the audience that they were watching the shapes of horses and jockeys parading, with the Grand Stand as a background, the murmur grew to a round of applause.

Admittedly, the images were far from perfect, but horse and rider were definitely recognizable . . . . The audience then watched the horses canter by as they hastened to the starting post, and despite the flickering and occasional blurring, everyone present began to dwell on the possibilities opened up by the "miracle" now being performed before their very eyes. Calls for the inventor were persistent, but when Mr. Baird was at last persuaded to show

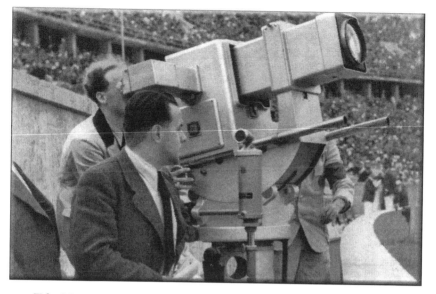

Television cameras make their appearance at the 1936 Berlin Olympics.

himself on the stage, he was too excited to speak. He had scored a triumph, and left it at that . . .

The first sporting event—with human athletes—ever to be televised to a mass viewing audience also happened to be one of the most infamous Olympic Games in history: the 1936 Berlin Olympiad, held between August 1 and August 16 under the menacing auspices of Adolf Hitler and his Nazi Party.

There were precious few privately owned TV sets in Germany to receive the broadcasts from the Olympic Stadium. Instead of broadcasting only to those handful of households with televisions (mostly belonging to high-ranking Nazi party members), twenty public TV parlors were installed throughout Berlin. About 160,000 viewers visited these parlors to watch the Olympics. At the stadium, three electronic cameras were used in conjunction with film cameras, and an "intermediate film" method sent exposed film from the cameras into the truck below to be instantly developed, transmitted a minute later to the TV parlors. Picture quality still wasn't ideal, but it was still a milestone accomplishment in the early history of television broadcasting.

Just over two weeks after TV made its official debut in America at the opening ceremony of the 1939 World's Fair, a college baseball game between Princeton and Columbia on May 17 became the first sports event to be televised in the U.S. The game aired on W2XBS, the experimental station in New York owned by NBC (and which would become WNBT, and finally WNBC). The game's on-air announcer was Bill Stern. But the single fixed camera and fuzzy image proved disappointing.

Television set owners were happier with the telecast of the Max Baer-Lou Nova fight held at Yankee Stadium a few weeks later, on June 7. And, later that summer, on August 26, W2XBS telecast the first major league baseball game on TV—a double-header, no less—between the Brooklyn Dodgers and Cincinnati Reds, at Ebbets Field in Brooklyn. Red Barber called the game, which had two cameras covering the action, but still resulted in several missed plays.

Once the television industry got on its feet properly after World War II, coverage of boxing, beginning in November of 1946, became an extremely popular and omnipresent part of the schedule. Within two years, prime time TV included boxing four nights a week.

Baseball attracted viewers in a big way for the 1947 World Series (between the New York Yankees and Brooklyn Dodgers), the first World Series to be broadcast. It aired only in the New York area, which had about 50,000 sets in use, but an estimated four million people watched at least part of the series. Remember, at that time, many television sets were not in private homes, but in neighborhood bars, restaurants, and other public businesses, where crowds were welcome to gather and watch TV as a community activity (while boosting profits for those particular establishments). It was reported that about 15% of televisions in the area were in bars and restaurants. "It is known, however," reported *The New York Times*, "that the World Series greatly stimulated the sale of videosets [sic] so that the current figures probably are appreciably higher." A Pulse survey showed that the TV audience for baseball games outnumbered radio listeners by 33 to 1.

As another result of television's swift rise in popularity, *Variety* reported

This 1939 ad for GE introduces a new era for the public and the company.

155

that Broadway theater box office suffered a 50 per cent slump during the World Series, with matinees suffering the worst, but business in bars with televisions rose 500%.

The first regularly-scheduled network sports program

Cavalcade of Sports began its network run on NBC in November 1946. Despite a title that implied an all-inclusive menu of sports coverage, it was actually devoted to boxing in its original version, as it broadcasted bouts from arenas in Manhattan on Monday and Friday nights. The Friday night installment was re-named *Gillette Cavalcade of Sports* and ran a total of fourteen years, eventually covering boxing bouts beyond the confines of New York, as well as other sporting events.

"Slo-Mo Replay" first used in TV sports coverage

In 1961, while on a business trip to Japan to secure rights to the Japanese All-Star baseball game, ABC's Roone Arledge had some spare time to take in a Samurai action film, which, to his delight, shot many of the fighting scenes in slow motion, giving them an almost eerie grace and fluidity of motion. He thought how great it would be to use slo-mo during ABC's NCAA football telecasts. He consulted with network engineer Bob Trachinger, who devised a crude process of videotaping the football action, and as it replayed, taping it again with another camera running at half speed. The initial results proved unsatisfactory, but Trachinger continued experimenting on his own time, and three months later presented the new, improved slo-mo replay innovation to Arledge. It was first used during a low-scoring Thanksgiving Day game between Texas and Texas A&M. So, with only a single field goal to replay at halftime, Arledge decided to put the slow-motion version on the air. "The picture still had some flicker," he wrote in his memoir, "but we showed something that had never been seen before. The following weekend, when Boston College quarterback Jack Concannon broke loose for a seventy-yard scoring run against Syracuse, we showed its potential. At halftime, once more we showed Concannon scoring in slo-mo—with dreamlike grace this time, [announcer] Paul Christman explaining every juke and jink. Watching, I saw the future open up before me."

First use of "Instant Replay"

During a 1955 Canadian hockey broadcast called *Hockey Night in Canada*, producer George Ratzlaff of the Canadian Broadcasting Corporation used a kinescope replay during a game, i.e. using a film camera technique (the advent of videotape was still a year away). The replay appeared on home screens—not instantly, but several minutes later.

The first televised sporting event on American television to use true instant replay was the Army-Navy football game on December 7, 1963 (the game had been postponed for a week, due to the Kennedy assassination). The CBS network's young Sports Director, Tony Verna, who directed coverage of the Rome Olympics in 1960, devised a videotape system using a 1,300-pound machine that enabled a play to be re-played in real time, only seconds after it took place live. But technical difficulties prevented the system from being used until the game was nearly over. When Army scored a one-yard touchdown that brought them to within six points of Navy, the instant replay was then used, but immediately created confusion among many viewers, who thought they must have been seeing things, as they had seen the exact same play occur before. Broadcaster Lindsay Nelson needed to quickly explain that Army hadn't just scored *again* (the final score: Navy, led by future Hall-of-Famer quarterback Roger Staubach, won 21-15).

The first Olympic Games to be televised in the U.S.

The 1936 Berlin Olympics were the first ever to be televised—albeit only in Germany—and the 1940 and 1944 Games were cancelled due to the war. Subsequent Games after the war were seen on American TV only as newsreels and limited highlights on news broadcasts. It wasn't until 1960 when American viewers saw CBS televise same-day (but *not* live) reports from the Winter Olympics in Squaw Valley, California. Originally, ABC paid $50,000 for the rights to cover the games, but later backed out. Roone Arledge, one-time president of ABC Sports and ABC News, explained, "CBS had picked up the Games, not out of any love for the Olympics but as a favor from [CBS president] Bill Paley to Walt Disney." What did Walt Disney have to do with it? He was chairman of the Pageantry Committee, responsible for the opening and closing ceremonies, and Paley was glad to ensure that his friend's efforts would be televised coast-to-coast.

The reporters covering these games included Walter Cronkite (still two years away from assuming his role as anchor of the evening news), Bud Palmer, and future ABC stalwart Chris Schenkel. But the CBS coverage was nothing like what American viewers today are accustomed to seeing for each winter and summer Olympics. The Squaw Valley broadcasts were initially limited to 15-minute recap segments each evening, beginning at 11:15 p.m. This obviously precluded the opportunity for any younger viewers to see the highlights, and also didn't allow for in-depth reporting on the individual events or the participating athletes. The *New York Times*'s television critic Jack Gould reflected the views of those who saw a squandered opportunity. "For an event that occurs only every four years and is a matter of international interest," he fumed, "it borders on ludicrous that only fifteen minutes a night should be allotted to the games . . . To assume that a day's multiple list of events can be compressed into a visual account of ten minutes or so may make economic sense to a broadcaster, but it can only be regarded as foolhardy by the winter sports fan." However, CBS did expand its coverage later in the week to include figure skating, hockey, and ski jumping, prompting Gould to eat some crow and later backtrack his criticism. "These events were part of the original CBS plans for the Olympic coverage, not an afterthought," he conceded in a follow-up column, "so that viewers who legitimately complained about those earlier 15-minute summaries, including this corner, were perhaps too quick in their judgments."

Later in 1960, CBS also offered limited coverage of the Summer Olympics in Rome. This was still before satellites enabled live broadcasts from abroad, so films of the Games had to be flown to New York for broadcast.

By the 1964 Tokyo Summer Olympics, NBC used the Syncom 3 satellite for its coverage, including live, color broadcasts of the opening and closing ceremonies. These were the first color transmissions via satellite from overseas to the U.S. (but only the ceremonies themselves were shown in color).

Chapter 7
Miscellaneous Firsts

The first TV commercial

In 1941, the FCC approved the licensing of commercial television, allow-ing advertisers to help foot the bill for the production and broadcasting of programming, such as it was at that point in television's history. In May of 1941, the National Association of Broadcasters estimated that there were only about 7,000 TV sets in use throughout the entire country (although other estimates have varied considerably), with most of those in the New York City area.

The commercial licenses went into effect on July 1, at which time about twenty stations in the nation became eligible to receive revenues from on-air advertising. But on that particular day, only the NBC station in New York (which had changed its call letters from W2XBS to WNBT), included any commercial advertising.

Just before the Brooklyn Dodgers-Philadelphia Phillies game that after-noon, a one-minute commercial for Bulova clocks appeared on the screen, consisting merely of a standard test pattern card with the moving hands of a clock overlayed, accompanied by the Bulova name. The story has often been repeated that this was only a 10-second spot. But printed accounts at the time report the commercial as running for a full minute, twice that day: the first airing immediately preceded the 2:30 p.m. broadcast of the Dodgers-Phillies game, and the second aired late that same evening. There is no concrete evidence that the spot included a voiceover.

As *Broadcasting* magazine reported, "Bulova Watch Co., New York, opened and closed the day's transmissions on this station with a visual adaptation of its familiar radio time signal. This two-program contract also provides television's first success story, for following the opening day's test the sponsor immediately signed up for daily time-signals for the standard 13-week period." The ads were to be shown six times a week for that 13-week stretch.

Later in the day on July 1, Sunoco began its sponsorship of the Lowell Thomas news program—which was basically a simulcast of his radio program. The only visual component consisted of Thomas seated in front of a microphone at a desk, surrounded by stacks of Sunoco oil cans (product placement on TV was no more subtle then than it is now). The last program aired that day was a one-shot TV version of radio favorite *Truth or Consequences,* sponsored by Ivory soap.

While the Bulova commercial is most commonly credited as being the first on television, at least two other examples can be considered, although they were aired at a time when it was not yet legal to include advertising on TV. In July of 1928, W3XK in suburban Washington, D.C. (the same station to first institute regular programming five days a week) aired a commercial, but was subsequently fined, and did not repeat the offense. On December 7, 1930, W1XAV in Boston included a program sponsored by I.J. Fox Furriers, and, like W3XK, was fined for airing the ad.

The first song ever sung on TV

As described earlier, the first television broadcast for public viewing in the U.S. originated in the G.E. labs of Schenectady, New York, on January 13, 1928. Among the individuals who addressed the transmitting apparatus during that historic two-hour program was WGY radio announcer Louis Dean, who decided to treat the handful of viewers to his rendition of "Ain't She Sweet," accompanying himself on ukulele. The song was written and published in 1927 by Milton Ager (music) and Jack Yellen (lyrics), and has since been recorded by musical giants such as Pearl Bailey, Frank Sinatra, and even the Beatles (Ager and Yellen scored another hit in 1929 with "Happy Days

Are Here Again"). Dean's rendition of the song, while most likely not on par with the above vocal legends, was nonetheless the first singing performance ever televised.

The first person ever to be censored on TV

There were few stars in show business bigger than Eddie Cantor when he became the first entertainer ever to be censored on live television. This occurred in the spring of 1944, as television was still emerging from its enforced period of inactivity during the early years of World War II.

On May 25, Cantor took part in an NBC music variety broadcast, seen on a direct hook-up between WNBT in New York and its Philadelphia affiliate. He was scheduled to perform the song "We're Having a Baby, My Baby and Me" from his 1941 Broadway show *Banjo Eyes*. According to Cantor, he and his singing partner Nora Martin were originally led to believe that the song selection would be fine for the broadcast. But just forty minutes before air time, NBC executives declared some of the lyrics unsuitable. The most troublesome passage was the following, which wasn't part of the actual, written lyrics, but rather spoken as a break in the song:

Girl: Thanks to you, life is bright. You've brought me joy beyond measure.

Boy: Don't thank me. Quite all right. Honestly, it was a pleasure.

Girl: Just think, it's my first one.

Boy: The next one's on me.

With no time to rehearse another number, Cantor and Martin performed the song without changes on the broadcast anyway. During that particular spoken exchange in the performance, however, Cantor's audio was cut off, and the camera focus was deliberately blurred to obscure his hand gestures and hula-like dance for comic effect.

After the broadcast, Cantor declared, "I'm blazing mad at the fellows who tell you it's all right and then sneak around and cut you off. Of course, NBC has the right to say we don't use the lyrics, but when little Hitlers tell you you can't do it just as you're going on, that's tough."

NBC vice president Clarence L. Manser explained that the portion of the song was censored due to "the obligation of NBC to the public to make certain that its facilities do not bring into American homes material which the audience would find objectionable." Just what exactly was supposed to have been objectionable about the song and/or Cantor's rendition remains a mystery.

Manser added that Cantor had been previously reined in by network censors, but the comedian claimed no recollection of any previous incident. He was also offended on a personal level by the notion that he had done or said anything in poor taste, considering the pride he took in using only clean material. "No man can be in the business for thirty-five years and do any vulgarity and last," he said. "I've been at it longer than NBC or television."

At least Cantor decided not to hold a grudge, or he may not have agreed to become one of the original rotating hosts of NBC's *Colgate Comedy Hour* in 1950.

Ironically, in a 1952 episode of *I Love Lucy*, the news of Lucy Ricardo's pregnancy prompted husband Ricky to serenade her with "We're Having a Baby, My Baby and Me." But while the song finally had its first uncensored televised performance, the word "pregnant" was not allowed to be said on the air at the time.

The first wedding to be televised

It may not rank among history's most famous televised weddings, such as that of Princess Diana and Prince Charles, but on May 1, 1931, television engineer Frank Du Vall married Grayce Jones at station W2XCR, owned by the Jenkins Television Corporation, on Fifth Avenue in Manhattan. The audio was carried by WGBS radio. The ceremony was officiated by Rev. Dr. A. Edwin Keigwin, Pastor of the West End Presbyterian Church, in front of a microphone and two televisor units.

The first telethon

Milton Berle's staggering popularity as star of his *Texaco Star Theater* program, beginning in 1948, made him an ideal choice to head American television's first telethon on April 16, 1949, for the Damon Runyon Memorial Cancer Fund. The 16-hour broadcast raised more than $1 million, with Berle himself reportedly—but unlikely—answering thousands of phone calls himself out of 16,895 total calls from the New York area. An estimated 50,000 calls came in from combined affiliates. A year later, Berle repeated his hosting chores for the same charity, in a 19-hour telethon (with a 2 ½ hour break), viewed in twenty-five cities.

In November 1949, the United Cerebral Palsy Fund ran a 14-hour telethon, and the following month, the Sister Kenny Foundation held a 5-hour telethon, hosted by Morey Amsterdam.

As for the most famous telethon of all, the MDA (Muscular Dystrophy Association) telethon, also known as the "Jerry Lewis Telethon," grew from several public appeals made by Lewis and then-partner Dean Martin on various radio and television programs in the early 1950s. They had been asked by New York businessman Paul Cohen to help spread the word about MDA's fundraising needs. The team continued to take part in one-shot television specials to raise money for the charity, including a 1956 telethon (even though they had recently split by then). Lewis hosted his first solo telethon the following year, and another in 1959. He resumed hosting the telethon in 1966, which aired only in New York. In 1971, the MDA Labor Day Telethon became a national telecast, eventually reaching about 200 affiliates each year—as many as each of the major broadcast networks.

The first interactive TV show

Interactive television takes several forms—from home shopping channels, from which viewers can order an item as it's being displayed or demonstrated on the air, to elaborate, Wii-enhanced video games—and anything else by which the viewer takes an active part in the screen image rather than just watching it passively. The first interactive program was actually a children's program called *Winky Dink and You* (or simply *Winky Dink*), which premiered as a morning show on CBS in October 1953, and ran for four years.

The show, hosted by Jack Barry, invited young viewers to become tangibly involved in the adventures of Winky Dink, a cartoon boy (voiced by Mae Questel, better known as the voice of Olive Oyl and Betty Boop) who would encounter a difficult obstacle at least once per program, necessitating the kids at home to help out. Alas, they couldn't do so unless their parents had first purchased a special Winky Dink kit, which contained a set of crayons and clear plastic sheet to be placed over the TV screen, and held there by static electricity. As an episode's story played out on the screen, Winky would inevitably encounter a physical obstacle or two. If he were walking through the woods and needed to cross a stream, viewers were asked to draw a bridge with their Winky Dink crayons on the plastic sheet affixed to the screen to help Winky get across.

Despite this stroke of marketing genius, the idea tended to backfire, when children participating in the show wouldn't necessarily bother to place the sheet on the television screen before drawing on the picture tube with their crayons. Some parents also voiced concern over their children sitting in such close proximity to the TV for extended periods, fearing overexposure to radiation (such fears were proven to be unfounded).

It has often been reported that Microsoft founder Bill Gates has specifically acknowledged *Winky Dink* as being the first interactive TV program in history. In 2013, columnist and CNN contributor Bob Greene set out to find the actual source of this legend, but ran into a number of investigative dead ends. Eventually, he found John Pinette, formerly of Microsoft and now a Gates spokesman. Pinette did recall being present at a meeting, time and place unclear, in which Gates, with a Winky Dink box and plastic sheet by his side, briefly referred to it as "an early example of interactive TV" before making a formal presentation about Microsoft's efforts in television.

The first Emmy Awards presented, and the first aired on TV

The first Emmy Awards were presented on January 25, 1949, in Los Angeles, during a cozy ceremony at the Hollywood Athletic Club. The name "Emmy" began as "Immy," short for the TV camera's image orthicon tube.

Only six awards were presented that night, and most of those were associated with the local Los Angeles station, KTLA.

The awards presented were:

Most Outstanding Television Personality: Shirley Dinsdale (ventriloquist) and her puppet Judy Splinters. Like her mentor Edgar Bergen, Dinsdale had her own radio show before beginning her local weekday TV show.

Most Popular Television Program: *Pantomime Quiz Time.*

Best Film Made For Television: The Necklace on *Your Show Time* series.

Station Award: KTLA, for outstanding overall achievements in 1948

Technical Award: Charles Mesak, Don Lee Television.

Special Award: Louis McManus, for his original design of the Emmy.

The 7th Emmy Awards were the first to be broadcast nationally on March 7, 1955, with Steve Allen as host. For the next fifteen years, through 1970, the awards were presented from both New York and Los Angeles venues in shared telecasts.

The first drama series to win the "Best Drama" Emmy for three or more consecutive seasons

Playhouse 90 was the first drama to win three consecutive Emmys in that category, beginning with the 1957-58 season. This was a remarkable accomplishment for an anthology program, considering that each week's production involved different writers, directors, and casts. Some of *Playhouse 90's* most acclaimed presentations throughout its run included *Requiem for a Heavyweight, The Miracle Worker, The Days of Wine and Roses,* and *Judgment at Nuremberg.*

The other drama programs that have since won the Best Drama Emmy for at least three consecutive seasons are:

The Defenders (1961-62, 1962-63, 1963-64)

Hill St. Blues (1980-81, 1981-82, 1982-83)

L.A. Law (1988-89, 1989-90, 1990-91)

The West Wing (1999-2000, 2000-01, 2001-02, 2002-03)

Mad Men (2007-08, 2008-09, 2009-10, 2010-11)

The first sitcom to win the "Best Comedy" Emmy for three or more consecutive seasons

The Phil Silvers Show, often known also as "The Bilko Show" (and originally titled *You'll Never Get Rich*) won the first of its three consecutive Emmys for the 1955-56 season.

Other comedies, and the seasons for which they won Emmys in at least three consecutive seasons are:

The Dick van Dyke Show (1962-63, 1963-64, 1964-65, 1965-66)

All in the Family (1970-71, 1971-72, 1972-73)

The Mary Tyler Moore Show (1974-75, 1975-76, 1976-77)

Taxi (1978-79, 1979-80, 1980-81)

Frasier (1993-94, 1994-95, 1995-96, 1996-97, 1997-98)

30 Rock (2006-07, 2007-08, 2008-09)

Modern Family (2009-10, 2010-11, 2011-12, 2012-13, 2013-14).

The first program to be #1 in the
Nielsen ratings for five straight seasons

The A.C. Nielsen Company originally conducted surveys for radio sponsors. In 1950, the Nielsen ratings replaced the Hooper ratings for television.

All-time favorites such as *I Love Lucy, Gunsmoke, Dallas*, and *60 Minutes* could easily be mistaken as having each won the ratings race for five consecutive years, but they all actually fell short of this particular milestone (although *60 Minutes* was in the top ten for a record twenty-three straight seasons).

All in the Family, which took the TV viewing nation by storm in the 1970s, was the first program of any genre to maintain the top position in the Nielsen rankings for five consecutive seasons. The groundbreaking sitcom premiered on January 12, 1971, as a mid-season replacement, but didn't win much of an audience until summer reruns. That audience remained so loyal that the show ended the 1971-72 season as the #1 program on TV. It stayed atop the ratings through the end of the 1975-76 season.

All in the Family broke through nearly all established barriers in prime time sitcoms. In addition to the controversial social and political issues the program used as comedy fodder, it also pushed the limits of acceptable language, with Archie Bunker freely peppering his remarks with "hell" and "damn," and, of course, a derogatory word for just about every ethnic minority and religion. Producer Norman Lear, having boldly stuck to his guns despite misgivings by CBS, paved the way for television comedy in the 1970s to accurately reflect the way real people speak and behave. It bears repeating that the show was also the first American sitcom to be shot on videotape in front of a live audience, rather than on film. And, of course, it was the first sitcom to include the occasional sound of a flushing toilet.

It is not possible to overestimate the impact *All in the Family* has had on American television. Lear and his writers pushed the limits of network program content; the topics and language used on *All in the Family* were unheard of on American sitcoms. It was perhaps especially shocking following CBS's purge of such genteel, rural sitcoms as *Green Acres* and *Petticoat Junction*. But considering the tumultuous nature of American society and culture through-out the late 1960s and early 1970s, the time was right for a program to reflect all that was being experienced and argued about by everyday people. Lear adapted the show from the British sitcom *Till Death Us Do Part.*

The Bunker family members over time became fully drawn, with Archie emerging as one of the most complex characters ever to appear in a sitcom. Family arguments ranged from personal bickering, especially between con-servative Archie and his liberal son-in-law Mike ("Meathead"), to debates about Vietnam, Watergate, gun control, sexual issues, religion, feminism, racism, and other formerly taboo topics for sitcoms. Such potentially explo-sive subjects had been handled before on variety and satire programs from *That Was the Week That Was* to the *Smothers Brothers* to *Laugh-In.* But as far as sitcoms were concerned, *All in the Family* practically re-invented the genre. Imagine an earlier stalwart sitcom father like Ward Cleaver making some of Archie Bunker's crude pronouncements in front of June, Wally, and Beaver, and you can see how times had changed on TV.

In tribute to the popularity and cultural significance of *All in the Family,* Archie and Edith's living room chairs are now on permanent display in the Smithsonian Institution.

Only two other programs of any genre have since duplicated the feat of leading the ratings for five consecutive seasons: *The Cosby Show,* beginning with the 1985-86 season, and reality singing contest *American Idol,* which led the ratings for six seasons in a row, from 2004 to 2010.

The first British program to air in the U.S.

On May 7, 1950, *The New York Times* reviewed the program *Café Continental,* produced by the BBC in the U.K. between 1947 and 1953, and described it as "the first English television show to be seen locally on a regular basis", i.e. Thursdays at 10:30 p.m. on the NBC affiliate.

The anonymous reviewer was none too pleased with the entertainment value of this variety show, citing that, along with the mediocre acts parading in front of the camera, "the production of *Café Continental* is stereotyped and old-fashioned by American video standards, the camera merely being placed in front of a night club floor show." The biggest complaint was that too many commercials for a zipper manufacturer interrupted the flow of the show.

The Avengers was the first British series to air on an American network in prime time. In 1966, with the interest in British popular culture on the rise, ABC paid $2 million for twenty-six episodes of *The Avengers* (starring Patrick MacNee and Honor Blackman). This influx of American cash enabled the show to switch from videotape (which, using the British PAL format, wasn't compatible with America's NTSC broadcasting format) to 35mm film. The fourth season of the program, with new co-star Diana Rigg, aired on ABC between March and December of 1966.

The first magazine publication devoted solely to television

Television magazine, based in London, published its first issue in March of 1928, making it the first regular television publication in the world. As founder/editor Alfred Dinsdale wrote in the first issue:

> We might, perhaps, be criticized as being premature in introducing a journal devoted solely to a subject which has as yet hardly emerged from the laboratory. But television, while it is not yet available to the general public, has long since emerged from the realm of theory; it was demonstrated in this country over two years ago, and has since been accomplished over long distances both here and in the U.S.A.

In the U.S., the March-April 1931 issue of *Television News* magazine, edited by Hugo Gernsback, became the first such American publication devoted totally to TV. Gernsback's editorial in that debut issue, like Dinsdale's, acknowledged the perception that it might have been too early in television's development to warrant a regularly published magazine:

> It is admitted that we have as yet quite a stretch to cover before we will be enabled to push a button and "look in" on any program

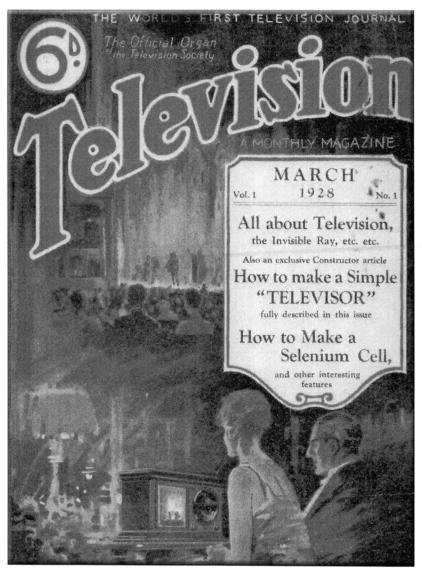

Britain's *Television* magazine, the world's first television periodical.

that is on the air. Yet an excellent start has been made; and the fact that there are now over twenty-seven stations broadcasting regularly should be indication enough that the new art is being taken more seriously, and that it is only a matter of time before the public will demand complete radio sets embracing the "visible" as well as the audible programs.

Up to the present time, there has been no regular periodical in this country to describe accurately from month to month the advances in television. It will be the mission of the new magazine to portray television from each and every angle and to show the reader what work has been done, not only in this country, but the world over.

Television News was folded into *Radio News* magazine in March of 1933. *Radio News* was founded in 1919 and published until 1959, before merging with *Electronics World* magazine.

An early national TV magazine, *Telecast*, premiered with its November 1949 issue, comprised of photo and written features documenting those early days of network TV. It did not survive long, but the date of its demise isn't clear. Other early TV magazines included *Televiser* and *Television* (both of which, if you've noticed, have proven invaluable to the research conducted for this book).

The best-known and most widely circulated television magazine, *TV Guide*, grew out of several regional magazines purchased by Walter Annenberg's Triangle Publications, and were then merged together to create a single, national publication. The first issue of *TV Guide* was published for the week of April 3, 1953. Lucille Ball's newborn baby, Desi Arnaz, Jr. graced the cover. As publisher Annenberg wrote in that first issue:

Television's growing importance in our daily lives brought a need for accurate and complete station schedules printed in convenient form . . . the new *TV Guide* offers readers throughout the Nation news, features, and columns by staffs of writers in the television capitals. As a national, as well as local magazine, *TV Guide* will make use of the most modern printing facilities, brining readers four-color pages—as a prelude to the day when television itself will be in color.

The first issue included reviews for programs *Robert Montgomery Presents*, and *Time to Smile*, a photo story on Walter Winchell, a piece titled "Stars Tell 'What TV Has Taught Me,'" and, of course, the cover story "Lucy's $50,000,000 Baby." Each subsequent issue's mix of local schedule listings and feature stories found immediate success with subscribers.

In 1980, *Panorama* magazine attempted to become a national news magazine covering the creative, technical, and financial aspects of network and cable TV. Think of it as *Time* or *Newsweek* for television aficionados. It did not include network or local program listings à la *TV Guide*, but instead presented both brief features and lengthy, in-depth interviews and investigative pieces, supported by ample artwork, photos, and eye-catching graphics. However, the ambitious publication lasted only sixteen issues.

And finally . . . The first book ever written about television
Now that you have read through Western Civilization's first book devoted solely to detailing television's "firsts," it seems appropriate to acknowledge the first book ever written about television.

In 1926, just months after John Logie Baird gave the first series of public demonstrations of his television system, the aforementioned Alfred Dinsdale, member of the Radio Society of Great Britain, wrote a small, 64-page book, *Television –Seeing by Wireless*. Published in London by Sir Isaac Pitman & Sons, Ltd., it was the first publication about the new medium for public consumption (not including technical manuals). Two years later, Dinsdale later founded and edited *Television* magazine.

In June 1932, Harper & Brothers published *The Outlook for Television,* written by *The New York Times* radio editor Orrin Dunlap, Jr., who chronicled both radio and television's development for the newspaper.

The number of television firsts has slowed considerably in recent decades, which was to be expected. Indeed, some observers are already predicting that television as we know it is on its way to obsolescence, as more on-line sources and subscription services gain popularity. And, while network television won't be disappearing any day soon, we might someday see a publication identifying the *last* of everything on TV. It may happen, but this author, and lifelong television addict, shudders at the very thought.

NOTES

Chapter 1: In the Beginning

Dinsdale explains definition of "television": *Television* magazine (UK) March 1928, p. 10.

... another human conquest of space." First TV station, Schenectady broadcast, *The New York Times,* January 14, 1928.

Sarnoff quote: "The television receiver, as at present developed . . ." Ibid.

"It is part of our policy to give our readers detailed technical descriptions . . ." Editorial, *Television* magazine (UK) March 1928.

"New Word" contest, *Television News* magazine, July-August 1931, p. 211.

"Queen's Messenger" story, *Television News* Sept.-Oct. 1931, p. 260.

Fannie Hurst and husband—first video chat: *Television News* magazine, July-August 1931.

Wynn quote: "A Jules Verne Comedian," *The New York Times*, December 6, 1936, sect. 12, p.14.

Lionel Barrymore talks about television: *The New York Times*, May 11, 1928, p. 30.

Milton Berle's first time on TV: *Milton Berle: An Autobiography.* Delacorte Press, NY, 1974, p. 121.

Television to doom legitimate theatre: Hugo Gernsback, *Television News* vol. 1, #6, Jan-Feb. 1932.

"Television is not a thing of the future . . ." *Radio Mirror,* "The Real Reason Mary Pickford Turned to Radio," December 1934, p. 12.

Eddie Cantor to memorize radio scripts: *The New York Times*, November 29, 1936, section XII, 12:1.

Opening of World's Fair televised: *The New York Times*, May 1, 1939, p.1.

War interrupts television in UK: BBC Yearbook, 1940 (p.13).

TV will be "insatiable monster": Thomas H. Huchinson, *Televiser* magazine, Fall 1944, page 13.

Chapter 2: Creative Firsts

"How We Staged the World's First Television Plays" by William J. Toneski, *Television News*, Sept.-Oct. 1931, p. 260.

"The Queen's Messenger" described by Michael Ritchie as "one of those high-society, European- setting melodramas ... " *Please Stand By*.

"The Queen's Messenger" as reported in *The New York Times*, September 12, 1928, page 1.

Hour Glass: "When the announcement was made ... " by Sidney R. Lane. *Television* magazine, October 1946.

Kraft Television Theatre, first regularly scheduled drama: *TV Guide*, March 1954.

Mary Kay and Johnny Stearns interview: Archive of American Television, August 25, 1999.

Variety review of *Mary Kay and Johnny*: October 13, 1948.

DuMont programs "have probably been more extensive and varied ... " *Televiser*, Sept.-Oct. 1945, p. 16.

"Only strong visual gags were used ... " "Turning Sound Programs Into Good Video," *Televiser*, Jan-Feb. 1947, p.16.

Radio writers study television: *Television* magazine, February 1946, p.46.

Martin Kane, Private Eye review by Jack Gould, *The New York Times*, September 11, 1949, Section 2, p. 9.

Appraisal of *The Goldbergs*: "CBS has come forth with such a format..." *Television* magazine, February 1949, p. 38.

The Goldbergs on Park Ave. commentary: *Television* magazine, April 1949. Gertrude Berg on writing for different media: *Television* magazine, June 1949.

Fred Allen quote about TV: *Television* magazine, December 1949.

John Carlisle and radio audience laughter: "To sit by a radio receiver and hear laughter…" *The New York Times*, July 24, 1932, section 9, p.1.

"Cavender is Coming" laugh track "was CBS's idea…" as explained by Buck Houghton, *The Twilight Zone Companion*, by Marc Scott Zicree, p. 288.

Alan Alda, M*A*S*H laugh track: *Panorama* magazine, February 1980.

Hal Linden, *Barney Miller* laugh track: *Panorama* magazine, November 1980.

"Should Television Have Studio Audiences?" Dr. Alfred Goldsmith, *Television* magazine, March 1946, p.19

Captain Video review: *The New York Times*, November 20, 1949, section II, page 9.

"We have to run through it to get the laughs out." *The New York Times*, March 26, 1950, section II, page 11.

Faraway Hill review: *Television* magazine, December 1946, p. 35.

Future for soap operas: *Televiser*, Jan-Feb. 1947.

"Has Daytime Video a Future?" *Televiser*, Fall 1944, p. 23.

"Programs during the day will have to be handled…" response by Norman D. Waters: Ibid., p.23

"Incredulous housewives and sleepy-eyed husbands…" "The Housewife Audience," *Televiser*, November 1949, p. 11.

"In the years to come, when historians are scribbling…" *Telecast* magazine, November 1949, page 30.

An American Family assessment in *TV Guide,* July 27, 1991.

"Viewers seemed to respond to almost any show…" *Panorama* magazine, September 1980, p. 49.

"I think we were getting a little bored…" George Schlatter, Ibid., p. 50.

"The problem seems to be…" Cyra McFadden, *Panorama* magazine, August 1980, p. 12.

The New York Times, October 10, 1947, p. 50 (World Series).

The New York Times, January 30, 1976 (John O'Connor story on *Rich Man, Poor Man*) p. 59.

The New York Times, November 26, 1991, p. D1 (HDTV).

Rich Man, Poor Man article, Les Brown, *The New York Times,* March 21, 1976, sec. II, p. 23.

Small Fry Club: ... the instrument suggests an intimacy..." *The Lucky Strike Papers,* p. 26, Andrew Lee Fielding. Bearmanor Media, 2007.

Dallas comic strip: Comic strips from TV series: *Panorama* magazine, June 1981, p.28.

Ben Casey: TV Guide, September 1962, as featured on www.TVObscurities.com.

Return of the Scarlet Pimpernel airs on TV: *The New York Times,* June 1, 1938, p. 21.

The Front Page review, *Television* magazine, October 1949.

The Boys From Boise – "We didn't have any recipe..." *Televiser* magazine, Winter 1945, p. 24.

The Boys From Boise review: Jack Gould, *The New York Times,* October 8, 1944.

Edgar Bergen on *Hour Glass: Newsweek,* November 25, 1946.

Pat Weaver interview, *Panorama* magazine, July 1980.

Richard K. Doan, "The Doan Report" *TV Guide* December 11, 1971. page A-1.

The Black Robe article, *Television* magazine, October 1949, p. 23.

Eddie Cantor prepares for TV: *Radio Mirror,* February 1939, p. 64.

DuMont refuses live audience for show: *Billboard,* October 30, 1948.

Chapter 3: Technological Firsts

First overseas broadcast—"He cleaned it up digitally and transferred it..." *The Times of London,* June 25, 1999.

Apollo 7 TV broadcast: *The New York Times,* October 15, 1968, p.1.

Jerry Fairbanks, *Television* magazine, November 1949, p. 27-28

Jerry Fairbanks, multi-camera system: *Television* magazine, March 1950 p.4.

Robert Dwan on filming *You Bet Your Life : The Secret Word is Groucho,* by Groucho Marx and Hector Arce, p. 56-57.

"Film on the Marx," *You Bet Your Life* filming technique : *Television* magazine, August 1952, p. 31.

Jay Leno describes his first VCR, *Leading with my Chin,* Harper Paperbacks, 1996, p.196.

First HDTV debuts in Japan: David E. Sanger, *The New York Times,* November 26, 1991, p. D11.

Chapter 4: First in TV News
Hunt for Lindbergh baby: *The New York Times,* March 4, 1932, p. 9.

The March of Time ". . . has the continuity desired for television." *Broadcasting* magazine, May 1, 1939.

Barbara Walters hired by ABC: *Newsweek* magazine, October 11, 1976, p. 68.

"On his own, Harry was excellent . . . " *Roone: A Memoir* (HarperCollins, 2003), p. 175.

"I can't think of an event of any importance ..." Don Karasik: *TV Guide* January 3, 1970.

"CNN is not very good journalistically." Edwin Diamond, *Panorama* magazine, September 1980, page 70.

"Any 24-hour news service can work ..." Roone Arledge, ibid, p. 30.

Chapter 5: First in Televised Political Events
Roosevelt's death, TV coverage: *Televisor* magazine, June 1945, p. 8.

First political broadcast: "The images that appeared on the screen . . . " *The New York Times,* October 12, 1932, p.48.

"Television not only covered but influenced the convention . . . " *Life* magazine, July 26, 1948.

Report of first televised Election night results: *The New York Times,* November 9, 1932.

Chapter 6: First in TV Sports Coverage
Japanese baseball game televised: *Television News* magazine, Nov.-Dec. 1931, p.331.

First use of Slo-mo: Roone Arledge, *Roone: A Memoir,* p. 38-39.

Roone Arledge, first Winter Olympics coverage, *Roone.*

Jack Gould's review of 1960 Winter Olympics TV coverage: *The New York Times*, February 19, 1960, p. 54.

Chapter 7: Miscellaneous Firsts

Cantor censored—*The New York Times*, May 27, 1944, p.17.

"Winky Dink and … Bill Gates?" by Bob Greene, CNN.com April 1, 2013.

BIBLIOGRAPHY

Books

Arledge, Roone. *Roone: A Memoir.* New York: HarperCollins, 2003.

Brooks, Tim, and Earle Marsh. *The Complete Directory to Prime Time Network and Cable TV Shows.* New York: Ballantine Books, 1995.

Brown, Les. *Les Brown's Encyclopedia of Television.* Detroit: Visible Ink Press, 1977.

Buckman, Peter. *All For Love: A Study in Soap Opera.* Salem, New Hampshire: Salem House, 1985.

Anchors: Brokaw, Jennings, Rather, and the Evening News.

Castleman, Harry, and Walter J. Podrazik. *Watching TV.* New York: McGraw-Hill, 1982.

Davis, Jeffery. *Children's Television, 1947-1990.* Jefferson, North Carolina: McFarland & Company, Inc. 1995.

Garner, Joe. *Stay Tuned: Television's Unforgettable Moments.* Kansas City: Andrews McMeel Publishing, 2002.

Harris, Jay S. (editor): *TV Guide: The first 25 Years.* New York: Simon and Schuster, 1978.

Lenburg, Jeff. *The Encyclopedia of Animated Cartoons.* New York: Facts on File, 1991.

Mitz, Rick. *The Great TV Sitcom Book.* New York: Richard Marek Publishers, 1980.

O'Dell, Cory. *Women Pioneers in Television: Biographies of Fifteen Industry Leaders.* Jefferson, North Carolina: McFarland & Company, 1997.

Paul, Michael and James Robert Parish. *The Emmy Awards: A Pictoral History.* New York: Crown Publishers, 1970.

Ritchie, Michael. *Please Stand By: A Prehistory of Television.* Woodstock, New York:

The Overlook Press, 1994.

Robertson, Patrick. *Robertson's Book of Firsts*. New York: Bloomsbury USA, 2011.

Schwartz, David, and Steve Yan & Fred Wostbrock. *The Encyclopedia of TV Game Shows*. New York: Facts On File, Inc. 1995.

Settle, Irving, and William Laas. *A Pictoral History of Television.* New York: Grosset & Dunlap, Inc. 1969.

Web sites
The Paley Center for Media web site.

www.earlytelevisionmuseum.org

www.obscuretv.com

Television Documentaries
"Television Under the Swastika" written and directed by Michael Kloft, produced by Spiegel TV, 1999.

"John Logie Baird: The Man Who Saw The Future" produced by Leman Productions for the BBC, 2001.

INDEX

47464824R00114

Made in the USA
Middletown, DE
25 August 2017